ONE STEP BEYOND

A Personal UFO Abduction Experience

ONE STEP BEYOND

A Personal UFO Abduction Experience

by

Elsie Oakensen

Regency Press (London & New York) Ltd.
125 High Holborn, London WC1V 6QA

ISBN 0 7212 0930 0

Printed and bound in Great Britain by
Buckland Press Ltd., Dover, Kent.

CONTENTS

Page

This book is dedicated to my family;
to my husband John for his loyalty throughout the initial traumatic
years following the sighting and his continuing support as time passes,
and I hope that our three sons and their wives and partners
Derek & Christine, David & Karel, Douglas & Rose
also our grandchildren Terri-Jayne, Anthony, Stuart,
Helen and Ethan
will look upon this as a record of one of the more
unusual aspects of the Oakensen Family History

AUTHOR'S INTRODUCTION

Ten and a half years after a UFO encounter an opportunity arose to make an appeal on television for contact with other UFO witnesses. As a result of this I met many very interesting people who offered suggestions for the reason why this strange experience should have happened to me.

The information which I gleaned was so full of surprises that it seemed sensible to record it all, not only as a biographical account of sixteen years of my life for the benefit of my grandchildren and my great-grandchildren, but also because I have since met so many people who have seen a UFO and have never felt able to tell anyone about it for fear of ridicule.

A 'Close Encounter of the Fourth Kind' as mine became known is so called because it involves an abduction and sometimes contact with alien beings. This has a traumatic effect on the witness who has come into contact with the unknown, and although there are now many UFO groups dotted around the country, there are still too many witnesses not knowing to whom they can turn for sympathetic and confidential counselling.

When I encountered a UFO on that memorable day in 1978, I had difficulty in finding someone to help me. It is estimated that five million people in Britain have seen a UFO. Each of them will be able to relate to some part of this story – and will then know that they are not alone.

ELSIE OAKENSEN

FOREWORD

Surfing on the rim

Of course, we all know that it must be crazy. There are no such things as UFOs, let alone extraterrestrials, so someone who dares claim that they have seen them close up has got to be deluded, or even making the whole lot up.

This is how it goes in the neat, ordered universe decreed to us by science. Except, science is not omnipotent. It has been spectacularly wrong before – and, I fear, it is pretty wide of the mark once again.

Indeed, science is not even quite so dismissive of alien entities as it seems to profess. If you took a poll of relevant experts there would be a heavy bias supporting their existence. Unfortunately, they are only happy with this closet admission when those aliens are conveniently far away – out there, somewhere, in the vastness of space definitely not coming here to effect our humdrum lives.

Millions of dollars has been spent probing the universe, straining to hear faint radio signals from some distant civilization, on the off chance that they may want to talk to us or that they would use such a primitive mode of communication even if they did. We, ourselves, have adopted radio for but a fraction of our lifetime as a thinking species and, in truth it is useless for talking to the stars, because it is limited by the snail's pace speed of light.

Send a message to even our nearest probable stellar neighbours and you may as well go away and make a pot of tea, for you will not get an answer for another nine or ten years!

About the one thing that these scientists are sure about in their mathematical deliberations is that these other intelligences are certainly out there – lurking in the infinite. All that is in doubt is whether we can ever find a way to breach the almost unimaginable distances that stretch across the cosmos and establish contact with these other souls. But the prize if you can beat the odds is enormous, for just imagine what they might teach us about science, medicine, philosophy, religion. Our world could quite literally change overnight if a message from 'them' were ever to be received.

Astronomers play merrily with toy telescopes, hoping against hope that this time they may pick up more than just the hiss of interplanetary static. But suggest that they may listen to a rather less monotonous UFO witness, or discuss the possibility that aliens could be much nearer than some distant star system – and the room goes very quiet.

Yet this desire to find aliens – this holy grail of science – may lie at the end of a simple phone call to a rational, intelligent witness – who could describe what these scientists have spent their lives seeking in fruitless endeavour.

The forlorn quest to chat with alien ham radio enthusiasts is not considered improbable enough to scupper massive budget plans that sanction the cosmic equivalent of hunting a needle in a haystack. In fact, that mythical search would be a doddle compared with finding alien radio messages in the great beyond. But – no matter – the fifty-year-old dream goes on without even so much as a 'hello' yet recorded to offer encouragement to its frustrated followers.

If UFOlogy were so pointless a task as that I would have given it up long ago – but then cosmology is respectable. UFOlogy is the province of the grade one loony.

So how about a time out? – you may well ask politely of these starry-eyed astronomers. Why not look into that data scattered around them that tells us all about UFO contacts? In reply there is a cantata of clearing throats – fixed looks that suggest they have been peering down on optical lens too long – and the urgent plea – *send for the men in white coats and let's get back to the real world, please.*

In a sense this double standard applied by science when spending vast sums of taxpayers' money should be the source of more of an outcry than it is. For whilst radio astronomy is a very expensive luxury which can only be done with complex equipment that would sink the treasury of a small nation, research into UFOs is vastly less difficult to fund and can be (indeed is being) carried out by thousands of ordinary people without top heavy bank balances.

Yet – with one glorious exception (that of France) – UFO research is completely unfounded. Its practitioners scurry hither and thither, scraping together the bus fare or petrol money to chase after frightened witnesses, and its consequent standards of work tend to fall somewhere between not very good and downright awful. To compensate its groups of enthusiasts set up power-mad quangos, bureaucracies of the highest order (but often the lowest wit) – who are excellent at shuffling papers, so long as the papers never go anywhere, and any that do never say anything important.

As such – rightly or wrongly – this field is still regarded as peopled by the watcher after starships (inevitably piloted by little green men – to match the big green ones that run the UFO groups, who are incessantly jealous of one another – fighting star wars with each other's star witnesses). They all stand abreast in anoraks gazing off hilltops in some vain sense of expectation.

This is the popular myth – which is, of course, completely untrue (or maybe not). So what of the reality? Is it really quite so terrible as it seems?

Well – no – as you are about to find out within this book. There is hope for progress – perhaps not amongst the stuffed shirt scientists with their pompous idealogies, or amidst the tangled weeds of UFO groups that strangle one another via internecine warfare. Salvation may lie in the words of those who really ought to know what they are talking about – the witnesses to this mysterious phenomenon.

You will find that Elsie Oakensen is not a nutter, or a freak, or a dotty stargazer. What she tells you is what has happened to her, of that I have no doubt. Nor, I suspect, will you doubt it either after listening to her matter of fact presentation.

Elsie is a careful, thinking and caring individual with no predisposition to belief or disbelief, just a burning desire to understand what befell her that night on her way home from work.

Lest you think that this makes her unusual, let me assure you of one thing. I have been an investigator of UFO activity for over twenty years and in that time have confronted thousands of people such as Elsie (whom I have been fortunate enough to get to know). These were in Britain, Australia, the USA, eastern Europe – indeed many places – all of whom profess to have had a close encounter with this perplexing phenomenon, which in its most extreme form I like to call *spacenapping*.

These folk cover the whole range of human life – but they are above all, sensible, intelligent and almost paradoxically down to earth – far from the wide-eyed, egocentrics you might anticipate. These facts have been confirmed by several studies to be conducted by clinical psychologists or psychiatrists, almost embarrassed at having to publish reports in prestigious medical journals stating that these are normal folk – not spaced out crackpots. But they have no choice in that regard, because that's precisely what they are!

Nor are these witnesses generally desperate to see their name in lights or to appear on TV. Those who do go public think long and hard about the risks of such exposure and many is the time that I have been approached with the opening words – *I am not sure if I should tell you this, I don't want anyone else to know, please make sure you don't tell my husband/wife.*

In June 1992 I was invited to participate in a week-long symposium at the highly respected university of MIT – just across the Charles River from Boston, Massachussetts. If you doubt the impact of this prospect, remember that it is where physicist 'Sam Beckett' – in the TV series 'Quantum Leap' – supposedly got his skills to build a time travel device. So the very thought of MIT staging a symposium on UFO abduction was a very big deal.

The sessions ran all day and were held largely in camera, to protect the witnesses who told their stories but also to mask some of the dozens of scientists – ranging from physicists to psychologists who had conducted special research projects and presented their results at this gathering for the first time. Many of them were as wary as the spacenap victims of sacrificing their reputation to the maelstrom of media attention and public disrepute. But they risked it – and the outcome was perhaps the most positive step forward the subject has yet taken.

The proceedings alone ran to 700 pages of an encylopaedic book which comes with a free hernia for any postal worker brave enough to deliver it to your door.

One of the five papers that I presented at this epic event was a detailed statistical analysis of the fifty cases of alien spacenapping that I had delved into within the UK – Elsie's included. I had asked each of these witnesses if they wanted to go public and only three of them had. This immediately scuppers the erroneous view that these people are eager to talk (especially for money). Instead they often wish to goodness that this thing had never happened and tell others simply because they cannot live with bottling up what can be the most traumatic event of their lives. Or else they feel that the rest of society has a right to share in the wonders that they have seen.

Indeed, one psychiatrist in her study had noted that she could only find one other group of people who shared similar characteristics to those who experience a UFO close encounter. They too displayed a suspicion of others, a yearning desire to talk which was fighting strenuously against the feeling that this is something so personal that nobody else could possibly understand. They even sometimes felt self-depreciation – blaming themselves for what has taken place, even though logically they know that they were merely unfortunate victims in the wrong place at the wrong time.

Those other people identified by the psychiatrist are victims of rape – not exactly the image that would spring most readily to the mind of those of you lured into a false sense of disrespect by the wild trivialisation of our society when talking about UFOs. But once you have spent some time with these people, as I have been able to do, the analogy soon comes into true focus.

Those who encounter a UFO at close quarters are amongst the most misunderstood members of society. And all those who scoff must face the prospect that they could join their numbers in the blink of an eye – for these things do not happen to some and not to others. You are not mysteriously immune just because you don't believe it. It only takes a second to see a UFO and anyone can potentially become the next to find their universe falling apart.

If it does, I can assure you, not only will you suddenly understand what it takes to speak out as Elsie is doing in this book, but you will have a whole new perspective on the mysteries of life. For you will know – without doubt – that we do not even begin to comprehend the great unknown. There are giant questions which remain unanswered. But the first step towards ending this monumental riddle of the space age is to accept that there is a problem to be resolved.

Many theories are being studied by UFOlogists these days. Library shelves are full of them. They range from strange physical energies that can scramble peoples brainwaves, to metaphysical theories about the basis of life itself. They talk of 'aliens' who may really be us – perhaps visiting from our far future – or of creatures that come from another dimension exploring earth just as we investigate newly discovered species deep under the ocean.

Nobody knows what is really going on. But it is always best to pay heed to those who have met the mystery head on and come out the other side, for people like Elsie have a unique viewpoint to offer. They can provide the key to unlock the door that may let us peer into the wonders of the UFO mystery.

This book will open that door for you at least a crack. It will make you realise that there is a big question crying out to be answered – a question that all who scoff ignore at their peril.

The race is on to find the secrets of the UFO. Read this book and join the hunt.

JENNY RANDLES,
Fleetwood, Lancashire, June 1995.

ACKNOWLEDGEMENTS

I am most grateful to the following people and groups, for without their ongoing support and encouragement this book would never have been written.

To TED AND JAN LAWSON, my brother and sister-in-law, who originally put the idea of an 'article' into my head; JENNY RANDLES whose encouragement turned that idea into an interesting and rewarding exercise, who introduced me to all aspects of the media and has written the Foreword to this book; JOHN SPENCER who offered guidance along the way; also DERRICK BUTCHER AND RITA HUGHES who converted my handwritten notes into this presentable form.

To MEMBERS OF BUFORA AND NUFORC (too numerous to mention individually) for their support, co-operation and encouragement, also for advice when required; and especially to KEN PHILLIPS and the many other UFO Witnesses I have met at the WITNESS SUPPORT GROUP MEETINGS where we are able to express our thoughts and fears openly and know that they are understood.

To CICELY who typed the original report, copies of which are now on several continents; TREVOR THORNTON, JOHN ADDISON and MARK BROWN who investigated my sighting, also other members of UAPROL who later became involved; the FOUR LADIES FROM BYFIELD who had the courage to report the incident at PRESTON CAPES: to GRAHAM PHILLIPS, ANDREW COLLINS AND MARTIN KEATMAN who conducted the hypnosis session which was deemed to be necessary, and to PETER AENGENHEISTER, past editors and staff of the *Daventry Weekly Express* who, from 1978, maintained a balanced interest in the subject and whose reporting of it was always dealt with in a very sensitive manner. My thanks also to ANGELA MARSH and ANNE EDWARDS, my two impostors on the 'Tell the Truth' television programme; and to REG PINCKHEARD who introduced me to my first crop circle.

To GRAHAM ALLEN for answering my television appeal and proving to me that I was not alone, then with his mother VALERIE and GARY H, guiding me through the progressive stages in coming to terms with the situation; and ERNEST STILL, KATE BUTCHER, MONA CROSS, DAVID CLARK, PHILIP MANTLE and BOB DIGBY who encouraged me to speak publicly about the subject whenever an opportunity arose.

To CHARLES CHAPMAN and the many people I am now meeting, or working with, in order to develop my new vocation as a Healer.

Finally, I owe a great debt of gratitude to my very special friends JOAN and FRANK PEARSON who always had time to listen when I needed a friendly ear – and whose understanding kept me sane.

God Bless you all.
ELSIE OAKENSEN.

LIFE IS A CHALLENGE

Life is a challenge we all have to face
Living together in an appropriate place.
We all have a reason to be where we are
In the oceans, the earth – or perhaps a star.

We are all of us made in the image of GOD.
We each have a pathway no other has trod.
Have faith, have courage. In HIS footsteps do tread.
As you travel along you'll see HIM ahead.

HIS presence you'll feel. Within, you will glow
With a light that enhances wherever you go.
Great mountains, deep lakes, whatever you see
Were fashioned by you, LORD, to benefit me.

To inherit the earth was an honour bestowed
On each one of us who is travelling this road.
On guard are the Angels. The stars shine their light
And the end of that journey will soon be in sight.

From a spiritual writing which I received on 16 January 1995

WHAT FOLLOWS IS THE STORY OF MY JOURNEY

ELSIE OAKENSEN.

Chapter One

AN UNFORGETTABLE DAY

Over the years my married life was in many ways ordered by decisions made by the incumbent Chief Constable in the Northamptonshire Constabulary.

During John's term as a Constable the system was to transfer sometimes as many as thirty police officers on the same day to different parts of the county, all at the same time with each family group having been given about a fortnight's notice of the impending move. In our house chaos reigned as the day drew nearer and the final odds and ends were collected into boxes to be transferred to a new home, where new friends would be made and our three excited sons would attend another school for an indeterminate length of time. In our case it varied from a twenty-month stay in Wellingborough to one of eight and a half years in Kings Cliffe.

In December 1968 there was a transfer to Daventry on John's promotion to Town Sergeant and in 1972 to Wootton Hall Park in Northampton on promotion to Inspector at Mereway Police Station and around this time the County Police Officers were given permission to buy their own homes and allowed to travel to and from their points of duty if they chose to do so.

Back in 1955 after the birth of our sons, I had returned to the teaching profession and was, I believe, the first policeman's wife in the county to do so, something which was thoroughly disapproved of at that time in Police circles but which nowadays is a normal part of Police family lives. I had explained to the Northamptonshire County Education Committee that because of the short notice which we were given by the Police of any forthcoming transfers, I would only be able to give two weeks' notice as opposed to the normal two months which was expected from teachers towards the end of the term and a splendid working relationship followed.

Then in 1973 John and I decided to take advantage of the opportunity to buy our own house. At that time he was stationed at Mereway Police Station in Northampton and I was Deputy Head of Braunston C. of E. School. Our eldest son Derek was working with Beecham's Research Laboratories in Worthing and the youngest one, Douglas, was in the R.E.M.E. David was an articled clerk with an accountancy firm in Daventry, so on 2nd July 1973 he, John and I moved all our personal possessions into our new home at Church Stowe.

This was a very small village of about thirty houses with no streetlights, no footpaths, no shops and at that time there were only two buses a week to and from Northampton. We chose to live here because it was about three-quarters of a mile from the A5 and four miles from the M1. I always describe it as like being on holiday once you turn off the busy main road, so quiet and peaceful. It was then also about half-way between John's work and mine, each of us going in different directions daily and meeting up afterwards in those relaxed and peaceful surroundings.

This was the family life we enjoyed for the next five years. By then Derek had joined the Sussex Constabulary, David had qualified as a Chartered Accountant and was working abroad and Douglas was back in Civvy Street. John had been transferred back to Daventry Police Station, this time as Town Inspector and I had been promoted also, then being the Head of the Daventry Teachers' Centre where I organised in-service courses for the teachers working in the surrounding area.

We considered ourselves to be an ordinary working family. Since the boys were born I'd had a variety of full-time teaching posts following six Police moves, mostly to villages where wives in those days were almost as involved in Police work as were their husbands. Life for me was very hectic, demanding a great deal of organisation on my part and a great deal of co-operation from the rest of the family. But I did no more than many other working wives did then, or do now.

I had no reason whatever to believe that this kind of routine would change very much, if at all, until either John or I reached the point of retirement. I could not even envisage a change in my interests. My time was filled mainly with long hours at the Teachers' Centre and the rest was taken up with family commitments. My health was good and retirement at sixty was twelve years away.

22

Much of the annual holidays granted to teachers is spent preparing the following term's school activities and my work in the Teachers' Centre was no different, but in November 1978 I had an additional responsibility. I was involved with a group of young people who were researching into educational subjects as part of the Government's Job Creation Scheme and it was my brief in all that to help each of them find a permanent job if at all possible.

The Teachers' Centre was housed in a temporary building in one corner of St. James's Infant School playground and on the morning of the 22nd November 1978 I wove my way through a group of parents standing outside the school gate. They were watching their children in the playground before the school day began and as I edged my way through to the Centre I was sure that all was well with the world. The weather was fine, the sky blue and on the way to work I had taken my car into the garage for a service. Then, on arrival, I heard that one young man had been successful in obtaining a permanent post. What more could I want?

So completely unaware of what lay ahead, I suggested that at lunchtime we should have a Chinese meal to celebrate his good fortune. This was most enjoyable, but as we were preparing to leave the restaurant I felt a tightening sensation around my head and thought I was going to faint. Now what was I to do? How embarrassing it would be if I did. Quickly a decision had to be made and summing up the situation I thought that if this were so then it would cause less fuss if it happened in the restaurant than if I fainted in the street, so I sat still wondering what had caused it and whether I had eaten something which had disagreed with me. It was as if a band of material had been put across my forehead and around my head and was being pulled tighter and tighter. I'd had many types of headache before, I was used to them, but I had not experienced anything like this. It was certainly not a migraine, I knew that. This was all round my head and just above my eyes, a completely new type to me. I did wonder if anyone else was feeling as I did. I looked around but they were all enjoying their meal and the conversation going with it, so I did not ask. I was mainly worried for myself as I did not want to be an embarrassment to anyone there.

Suddenly it stopped as surprisingly as it had started. The pain which had lasted for only about a minute had disappeared completely and no one else seemed to have noticed my discomfort.

During this time the young man had been in the cloakroom, so I paid the bill and said nothing to him. We returned to the Centre in a happy and relaxed frame of mind, talking about his new job and his prospects for the future – and the incident in the restaurant slipped completely from my mind. There was no way at that time that I could possibly have known that it was to have a relevance to something which would happen later that same day.

After the day's duties were complete I phoned my husband to tell him I was leaving. We had this system whereby if he were not on duty that phone call indicated that it was time to put the vegetables on to cook as my journey would take about fifteen minutes.

During the day my car had been delivered to me at the Centre and at 5.15 p.m. I was ready to leave. There were no in-service training courses for teachers that day so I gathered up my belongings and locked the premises, then walked to the car and checked the lights. The left hand front side-light was not functioning. It had been a lovely day and wispy grey clouds were just appearing in the blue sky so, driving on dipped headlights, I started my journey home.

The section along the A45 from Daventry was quite uneventful and at the traffic lights at Weedon I turned right on the A5 to travel towards Towcester. Ahead of me I could see two very bright lights, one red and one green, immediately above the road along which I was to travel. My immediate thought was that this must be a very low-flying aircraft which would soon zoom over my head. But there were buildings on each side of the road between it and me and it seemed low enough to crash into them and then land on top of the car. I told myself to put my foot down hard on the accelerator pedal. With a bit of luck I would get under it before it crashed and still be alive to tell the tale when I arrived home. But it was of no use. There was a lot of traffic on the A5 at that time of day and strangely it seemed as if everything had gone into slow motion. That crash seemed inevitable but for some inexplicable reason I knew I would be safe.

I was convinced the crash would happen behind me. (It was not until twelve years later that someone pointed out that the landing lights on an aircraft are in the opposite positions to those I could see, so that if it had been a plane it would actually have been travelling in the same direction as I was and I would have seen it fly over the crossroads as I reached the traffic lights.)

Suddenly I realised that it was not moving at all. It seemed to be stationary and I travelled towards it with my nose practically pressed on

24

the windscreen. I knew that in the time I had before I drove directly underneath it I would have to collect as much information as I could about it. After all, I reasoned with myself, I was married to a Police Inspector and they are never satisfied with only half the facts. I would have to give a very detailed description when I recounted this particular incident.

I looked hard at it. In the darkening sky I could see a form which I would describe as a dumb-bell shaped aerial object with a brilliant red light under the left sphere and an equally brilliant green light under the other. It was grey in colour, blending in well with the grey wispy clouds accumulating above it and it appeared to be made of a very smooth plastic-type material. This 'thing' was considerably wider than the road, and was estimated later to have been about fifty feet in length and a hundred to a hundred and fifty feet above it.

As I approached it I could see no windows or openings anywhere and I felt compelled to stop and find out more, but the A5 was (and still is) a very busy trunk road. I could hear nothing unusual at that particular time and drove immediately underneath it. Had those two lights been over a field to the right or left of the A5 I doubt if I would have taken any notice but they were directly above the road just before the lay-by at the bottom of Stowe Hill.

Now, coming up to that point there were speedy decisions to be made. Should I stop on that lay-by, get out of my car and look up leisurely at that thing? In the split second that I had to decide, I realised that if I did swerve suddenly out of the line of traffic and stop, other drivers (whom I felt certain must also have seen it and perhaps would be in a shocked state like myself) would then be additionally surprised at my sudden move and an accident might occur. So I decided to continue with the flow of traffic and stop in a much safer place at the top of the oncoming hill. I needed to collect every piece of information that I could. That did seem to be very important at the time, but not important enough to cause an accident.

I drove past the lay-by and noticed that the traffic which I was meeting was not slowing down. I had expected it to do so because I thought that it would be impossible to travel along the road in that direction without noticing what was up there in the sky ahead of them. I looked into the inside mirror of the car but could see only traffic behind me. I passed the Clarke Bros. Garage and continued up the hill, but still could see nothing else whenever I looked back. I needed to know more and desperately hoped that I would soon be in a position to be able to do so.

To reach my home in Church Stowe I had to turn off the A5 at the top of the hill in this section of the road and by then I was completely intrigued by the sighting of such an extraordinary craft. After turning, the hill continues and there I was able to stop and look back. Here it was safe to do so and I wanted to see whether it was still in the same position over the A5. I gave a sigh of relief. It was – and at that point I was about level with it, being rewarded with a side view then as well as the one I'd had from underneath. I stood for a moment marvelling at its structure and noticing again the smoothness of the outline. What was this strange craft? I knew what it *wasn't* but could in no way find a word in my vocabulary to describe what it *was*! Then, as if to further attract my attention, the green light started to flash. "How strange," I remember thinking as I started the engine of the car, "Why did it do that?"

Wonder disappeared into the background and curiosity came into focus. Was it some kind of signal, and if so what was it signifying and to whom was it being sent? Was it for me? If so, why? Why would I think that it could be? Whatever would something like that want with me? "Who am I?" I asked myself but could only feel that I was nobody special, just an ordinary person on her way home from work, yet now my curiosity was really getting the better of me. Had the 'pilot' noticed that I was interested in it because I had stopped to get a better view? Was it now coming to satisfy my curiosity? I could not understand why but I really did need to have answers to those questions. Perhaps if I had been more psychically aware at that time I could have understood why it seemed to hold such fascination for me but that was to come later.

Church Stowe is a very small village high on a hill and travelling along the country road towards it I was able to look back and observe those two lights which remained in the same position. In that half mile or so of road I looked back three times and each time the green light was flashing but the red one was not.

About half a mile from the A5 I turned right into the village and it was here that I turned, as usual, in second gear, but when I changed up to third gear something most unusual happened. My foot was hard on the accelerator pedal which was then flat on the floor of the car. There was no sound from the engine at all. The car was slowing down and had almost reached the point of stopping. At that moment the strange object which I had driven under on the A5 was the farthest thing from my mind. My only thoughts at that time were far from polite and winging their way towards certain mechanics in a Daventry garage who had that day serviced my car. If it had been serviced properly, nothing like that should have happened.

The sensation of an accelerator pedal actually touching the floor of the car whilst it was moving was a new experience for me. I wasn't known for speeding. In fact I had often had my leg pulled for doing exactly the opposite thing, and this was an experience I could well have done without.

I took my foot off the pedal and depressed it again. The same thing happened and the car was definitely in the process of stopping. Now what was I to do? If it did come to a halt and would not restart I would have to push it on to the side of the road, walk home and ask John to look at it. He had been in the R.E.M.E. and worked as a mechanic before joining the Police. He would know what to do.

Believe it or not, I was actually brought up in a garage but here I was feeling absolutely helpless. Being a girl, I was never allowed to do more than find the right-sized spanner or whichever tool was needed whilst Dad did the repairs. However, I did later aspire to vulcanising patches on to tubes after my brother Ted had removed the wheel from the car. But that was only allowed during the time whilst Dad had volunteered for War Service with the Royal Observer Corps (as it later became known) at the time of the D-Day landings during World War II. On his return we all went back to square one and what goes on under the bonnet of a car still remains a mystery to me.

I thought of John and wondered what he would do in similar circumstances. Then I had what could only have been called an inspiration. I remembered how, when after Silverstone race days, he would always be asked what he did when he was on traffic duty and everything seemed to be coming towards him from all directions at the same time. His confident and unruffled answer was always the same. "YOU DON'T PANIC. You just stop everything, then beckon on the traffic from one direction at a time and eventually it all sorts itself out."

That attitude seemed appropriate for me at that very moment so I told myself not to panic but to start from scratch and see what happened. I did not switch on the engine (the red ignition lights were not on), I changed from third gear to first and depressed the accelerator. To my great surprise and relief the car started normally and I was able to continue on my way.

I offered up a silent prayer of thanks. But how short lived my gratitude was to be I did not realise. The car was behaving very well as I changed from first to second gear, then up to third gear again and I travelled happily along the next 100 metres or so of road. Here it was bordered on both sides by trees and the highest branches of these formed a canopy above the road, one which in autumn had been a blaze of colour but by then the leaves had fallen. Even so, the overhanging branches darkened the area and gave the impression of travelling through a tunnel.

Well! I remember reaching the end of the trees. Then the next thing I knew was that the car was stationary, the natural light had disappeared and everything was in absolute blackness. My engine had stopped. My lights were out. Everything was black, dark, velvety blackness. I knew I was sitting in the car, my hands were on the steering wheel but I could not see the car, the road, the buildings or the trees. I had no idea where I was at all. I wondered where all the lights had gone and how it could have happened so suddenly. I felt strangely calm and unafraid, then as I sat still I began to realise that some course of action would soon be necessary to remedy the situation, but what? I fumbled around for a torch, but could not find one.

Then suddenly, at that very moment, as if someone, somewhere was reading my thoughts, a brilliant white circle of light about a yard in diameter shone on the road to the left of the car by the passenger door. It lit up the road and I could see that the car was stationary beside the farm gate about fifty yards further on from the tree-covered part of the road – and that I had also travelled round a right-angled bend in that section of the road. That light went off and I sat in darkness again. Then another circle of light shone towards the left-hand front of the car and went out. Lights then continued to flash onto the ground, on and off, on and off, in a semi-circle around the front of the car from left to right, each punctuating the darkness and assuring me that I was still in the village and on my way home. This sequence was then repeated in a semi-circle in the opposite direction, from right to left back to where they started.

I was absolutely fascinated and sat watching as each one shone, taking into my mind the completely circular shape of each light as it lit up the road, its whiteness and its brilliance. I could not recall ever having seen any light so pure, nor yet so circular in shape. Then they repeated the route from left to right again and I began to realise that I was counting them too. The last one shone in the garden of the cottage to my right. It was then as if it was turned. It shone upwards from the garden to the roof on the front of the building and was switched off.

After the last light had gone out the whole area was in complete darkness. I have never seen Church Stowe in such darkness. It was absolutely black. Again I could see neither the houses nor the road, not even the car I was sitting in. Then as I sat in the darkness, astounded by this phenomenon, I calmly decided to try to analyse it all. I thought there had been fifteen light circles which had shone onto the road plus the one which shone on the garden. That one, for some reason, seemed to be more important than the others. I wondered why it had given me that impression? Was it showing me that there was something above the car at that point? I looked up again but could see nothing at all. So where had they come from?

My next thought was that perhaps someone was sitting on the roof of a building to my left and that he had a very powerful torch. Then I reasoned that if this were so then a beam of a yellowy colour would be visible from the torch, reaching down to a light on the road, which would be oval-shaped. But these lights had been completely circular and of a pure, brilliant white colour and there had been no beams at all to them. So, because of their shape they must have come from above, but how? And from what?

I was absolutely fascinated by all this and very curious. I looked upward through the car windscreen but saw only a blackness everywhere and expressing my surprise aloud, I said "Good Gracious." My car was stationary – but the very next moment, as if someone had pulled a switch, the enveloping darkness was replaced by natural daylight. I could again see the village and I was driving my car normally about thirty yards further along the road from the farm gate, in third gear as I had been when I reached the end of the trees.

I had not stopped my car by that farm gate in the village. I did not switch off my engine. I did not switch off my lights. I was not even conscious of being in control of my car from the end of the trees and around that right-angled bend. Yet the car and I were there. I cannot dispute the fact. Those perfect circles of light flashing on the road in a semi-circle around the front of my stationary car proved that to me. Had I not sat still watching them?

Then after they had gone out, I did not switch on my ignition. I did not put my car into gear. Nor did I depress my accelerator pedal and so start the car. I just found myself driving along normally. I can remember coming to the end of the tree-covered part of the road but I do not remember stopping. Yet I had stopped. I was stationary whilst the lights flashed around the front of me. After that I did not start my car, but I had travelled about 100 yards from the end of the tree-covered road, without being conscious of doing so. It had all happened as if by remote control.

I blinked my eyes and shook my head to make sure that I was not dreaming and to know that I really was in control of my car again. I changed down to second gear to negotiate the other right-angled bend in the village, this one by St. Michael's Church, and I was conscious of a feeling of relief as I drove round it knowing that in a few minutes I would have completed my journey home.

I drove straight into the garage, got out of the car and, not stopping to close the doors, I hurried through the backdoor and went into the kitchen where John stood preparing the meal. As I passed the cooker, I glanced at the clock. The time was 5.45 p.m. I said, "I'm just going to look out of the bedroom window, then I'll tell you something you won't believe." I rushed up the stairs and looked out of the window to where I had seen the red and green lights. I was expecting to see that strange craft in the sky but by then the clouds were thickening and all I saw was a yellow light flashing approximately where the others had been. Back in the kitchen I again noticed the clock and then realised that I was home later than I would normally expect to be. The journey had taken about fifteen minutes longer than it usually did.

The meal was served, whilst I related the details of my unusual journey home. John didn't say very much. I was disappointed. The police see many strange things on their travels and on that day I really did expect him to know all about it. He later described his reaction as 'stunned'. It was certainly in stunned silence that we ate our meal but then I wanted to talk. There were questions to which I needed answers, but he did not have any.

Fascination changed to frustration when suddenly, sometime after seven o'clock, I experienced another tightening sensation around my head exactly as I had done at lunch time. It also lasted for about a minute then stopped as suddenly as it had started. It was then I remembered the first one.

Why had this happened *twice* today, I wondered? I couldn't understand that at all. Could they be related? I had been trying to find an explanation for the other strange events that had occurred on that journey home, now here was another to add to them.

I had thought that having arrived safely home, albeit fifteen minutes later than expected, that that would be the end of it, but now I was wondering if those two identical feelings in my head were related to the journey in some way, and whether the whole experience was one which lasted over a longer period than I had originally supposed. That one at lunch time could have been the beginning of it all and the one I had just had could (hopefully) have ended it.

There were so many things buzzing around in my head that evening, things which I could not understand. I was not frightened of anything that had happened, but very puzzled, and my way of dealing with a situation like that is to put everything into some kind of order and analyse each aspect logically. So I listed them all and was amazed when I realised how much help I would need to find a solution which would satisfy me.

Before the evening was through I had compiled the following catalogue of questions:

- Was there any connection between those two tightening sensations I'd had around my head that day? If so, the first one could not have had anything to do with that Chinese meal. So, were they linked to the sighting and that strange encounter?
- What was that 'thing'? Was there someone somewhere who could explain what it was and why it was there?
- How could it have been suspended in the air like that? It was not a hot air balloon, an airship nor a helicopter.
- Had anyone else seen it, motorists on the road at the time, or local people? If not, was I selected in some way? How could I find out?
- Why had the green light started to flash as I looked back at it? Was it a signal? Was it telling me that it was aware of my curiosity towards it?
- Why did the electrics on my car fail? Was this anything to do with the 'thing' or did the car have a mysterious electrical fault? It had been in the garage that day for a service and had functioned normally before and after the encounter. In fact the faulty side-light bulb was working properly afterwards.
- How did the car (and I) get from the end of the tree-covered part of the road to the farm gate? I was not in control of it and it had negotiated a right-angled bend in the road.
- Why had my car stopped? Was it under the control of that 'thing'? Were any other cars stopped?
- What caused the natural daylight to change to complete darkness

where I could not even see the car in which I was sitting?

- Were those brilliant white flashing circles of light from above? If so, from where (or what) and why were there no beams? Were they linked to the car stopping or the missing time? If so, how and why?
- Why was I not afraid during any of these strange happenings? Had I been conditioned in some way? And if so, when?
- What was the yellow flashing light in the sky? Was it signalling 'Mission accomplished!'? If so, what was that mission?
- And the most intriguing question of all – What happened during the missing fifteen minutes – and why?

In bed that night I tossed and turned. Sleep would not come. My mind turned over the possibilities and probabilities for the strange happenings of that day. My hopes were high for a solution to it all but where to begin I did not know. I eventually fell asleep in a state of exhaustion, but before doing so I decided that I would have to tell as many people as possible about it to see if any of them could come up with a suggestion. That at least would be a start and I could follow each step to see where it led.

By no stretch of the imagination on that day could I possibly have realised what an interesting project it would turn out to be, and how from each suggestion would come a new experience which would open up a very different pathway along which I was to travel. Each pathway at the start followed a different direction, then sometime later they would become entwined and I was to find that finally they culminated in a most wonderful experience.

Chapter Two

ACTION AND REACTION

Now what was I to do? Obviously the immediate need was to find answers to my questions, the two most important being to find out what it was that I had driven under and whether anyone else had seen it too, but how to do it was another matter entirely.

I arrived at the Teachers' Centre at 9 a.m. the next morning and by no stretch of the imagination could I be described as carefree, as I had been the day before, even to say I was excited was not really accurate either, but anxious to report it to someone who may have seen it, or something similar, was definitely true. Cicely, my secretary, and the young people in the Job Creation Team had already arrived, so I decided to try my story out on them and note what reactions were forthcoming. This, I had decided, was a good place to start.

"Let's start the day with a cup of tea," I said as I walked in, "I need some advice and perhaps in your travels you will have heard of someone who can help me."

The tea was made and I told everyone present what had happened to me during my homeward journey the previous evening. I don't remember how long it took but they listened eagerly. I described the 'thing' (as I decided to call it) in detail. It was still unidentifiable to me, not a plane, an airship, nor a helicopter, also it was stationary and completely silent as far as I could tell.

"Oh, that's a UFO," said the young man I had taken out for lunch the day before.

"A UFO," I said with complete surprise. "What's a UFO?"

"An Unidentified Flying Object," he replied.

Now this was a subject about which I knew nothing. I had never heard John or any of the boys mention it either. He told me that lots of people had seen UFOs, but neither he nor anyone else in the group knew of anyone to whom I could speak about it. Then someone suggested a good place to start might be with the local newspaper reporter, with whom we had a very good relationship. So that became my next priority.

Peter Aengenheister, who was then a reporter at the Northampton Chronicle & Echo's Daventry Office, listened with interest and made copious notes. As far as he knew no-one else had reported seeing my 'UFO', but it could have been reported elsewhere by any of the motorists on the A5 at that time, when they had completed their journeys.

Peter wrote a report for his newspaper, which I read before he sent it off. He explained that he did not know how it would be received in Northampton, also that he had no control over the heading which would be given to the article.

At the time I wondered why he emphasised that point. I assumed it would be just a usual report of something strange. My ignorance at that time about the sensationalism of the subject by the media astounds me now.

Back at the Teachers' Centre thought was still being given to UFO groups. No-one had heard of any. John was making enquiries at the Police Station during his tour of duty and came home later with a telephone number of a society in Milton Keynes.

As a member of the Police Force he had always advised me and our teenage sons that if ever we were involved in an accident to write down as soon as possible an account of what had happened, so that if we ever needed to refer to it at a later date we would have the facts at our fingertips. This proved to be excellent advice. Cicely, the Centre's Secretary, had first class qualifications in shorthand and typing. I related the details of my experience to her. She took it down in shorthand and produced a beautifully typed account which was to be invaluable to me over the years to come.

One amusing incident later came to light as a result of this. I began to find that copies of this report were winging their way in many different directions unauthorised by me. One rather enterprising young man had, quite unbeknown to me, actually removed my name from a copy he had acquired and inserted his own. I only discovered this at a meeting we both attended where the Law of Copyright was being explained. Another colleague realised what had been done and quickly remedied the situation much to his embarrassment.

Peter's report was printed in the bottom left-hand corner on the front page of the *Chronicle & Echo* newspaper dated the following day and headed 'UFO blamed as car cuts out.' If the actual experience of that journey two nights before had not changed my life then this certainly did.

Many people, including a man named Reg Pinckheard, who I was to find in years to come was very knowledgeable about UFOs, called in to the Teachers' Centre to talk about it. My phone rang continually with people wanting to tell me of their experiences, or to hear more about mine and one of those was a lady with whom I later became acquainted through another group. Joan Pearson with her great interest in UFOs, spiritualism and corn circles became a very good and understanding friend to me

A lady I met in a Daventry shop spoke to me after seeing the report of my sighting in the newspaper. She was very eager to tell me about some lights which she had seen in the sky as she drove in Warwickshire several years before. These lights had paced the car for some distance as she travelled, then had 'shot off' and 'gone out'. She said she had never told anyone about this before because she couldn't prove it and feared ridicule – and now that I had had the courage to report my experience publicly she was so relieved to talk to someone about it who would understand.

But I didn't 'understand'. My aim in talking to the Press was a very blinkered one. I was only trying to find someone who had seen what I had seen – nothing more. But there was I listening politely to her. Why was she telling me this? What connection was there here? I had read about strange lights being seen near Long Buckby a few weeks before, and over Duston in Northampton, but could still see no connection with what had happened to me. I, very mistakenly now I know, was only looking for someone who had had the exact experience (or a similar one) to mine – a dumb-bell shaped UFO (as it was now being called) with a red and a green light shining from underneath its spherical ends. But listening as readily and eagerly as the opportunity arose, I could find nothing to which I could relate, such was my naivety at that time. That lady's relief was so great. She had been hoping to find someone to talk to for so many years.

Of my colleagues at that time the one I felt would be the most help to me was a physics teacher, and for some reason I was sure that if I told him what had happened he would have an explanation for it all. He listened politely to what I said but soon made it obvious that what he had heard did not come under the heading of 'physics', not as he understood it anyway.

But what did come from that conversation was an understanding of the reason why the lady in the Daventry shop had not told anyone about her 'lights'. I realised from the reaction I received from him that I would have to be very selective in my choice of people to approach for a 'sympathetic hearing'. Not that sympathy was what I was looking for. I, like her, also wanted someone who would understand what I was talking about. Someone – anyone – who would say to me, "I saw it too", so that we could compare notes. That was the only thing I wanted to happen, then I would be able to put it into the background and get on with my ordinary, everyday lifestyle. But as time went on it became obvious that this particular pathway would be across very stony ground.

I attended a Parish Meeting in Church Stowe shortly afterwards and Tony Fielden, the Chairman, suggested it should start with an account of my sighting, "as," he said, "that had been the most exciting thing that had happened in the Parish since the last meeting." Everyone listened, some with disbelief, but no-one was really rude. I could understand by then how they felt. I had not given UFOs a thought before that November day, maybe my reaction would have been one of disbelief if it had happened to someone else who was telling me.

At the time, those of us in charge of the five Teachers' Centres in the county met regularly with the Inspectorate. At the next meeting I was again asked to relate my experience before the meeting started. Here I met with a whole range of reactions from roars of laughter to helpful suggestions as to what may have caused the lights. Theories were put forward and suggestions made which were able to be discounted or remembered for future reference as possible answers. This was a very helpful exercise which prepared me for the reactions (sympathetic, understanding, ridiculing and downright rude) which were yet to come, but I knew what I had seen and what had happened to me and I did not understand it any more than they did.

I telephoned the number provided by the local police and it was that of a member of the Milton Keynes Astronomical Society who put me in touch with the Society's Chairman. He suggested that I should contact Ken Phillips who manned the 'UFO Hotline'. That I did and Ken explained that they had a small group of experts in all walks of life who conduct interviews with 'Close-Encounter Cases', that the witnesses are closely questioned, then colleagues in London and Manchester study the reports. He was talking about the British UFO Research Association (BUFORA) and the work of its investigators and researchers. This was the first time that I had heard of this organisation and at that moment did not realise its relevance, but I can see now that that phone call opened up yet another pathway which was to have a very influential effect upon my life at a much later date. I was quite excited at the thought that I would now meet people who would understand what had happened and would be able to give me a straightforward answer. How wrong I was!

Following this conversation Ken contacted a colleague in Leeds. The nearest BUFORA investigators to me lived in Leicestershire and it was Trevor Thornton who rang me and arranged an interview. This was to involve the filling in of two report forms, close questioning regarding the incident and scientific examination of the areas involved. He told me that at that time there were many sightings being recorded in Northamptonshire and that he had also arranged to see a Northampton man regarding a sighting which he had had the previous week and which sounded rather like mine. He, like Ken, also explained that if you have experienced a 'close encounter' (the term now being applied to my case) and you are worried or have received ridicule because of it, by speaking to a UFO investigator, you will find that you are not alone. Everything is handled sympathetically and in confidence, if you wish, and these people put your feet squarely on the ground again. The ball was now rolling in that direction and hopes for an explanation were high.

My brother Ted had spent sixteen years in the RAF and was at that time working with Air Traffic Control at Heathrow. I phoned him and told him my story. He was as interested and fascinated as I had been and suggested I should send a copy of the report to the Ministry of Defence. This I did and I received a very formal reply thanking me for doing so.

Whilst in the RAF Ted had a friend named Jack Pearcy who had a brother who was interested in UFOs. He lived in Devon and it was suggested that I should also send him a copy of the account of my sighting. Looking back I can see that he and Ken Phillips were both instrumental in bringing the 'Church Stowe Sighting', as it was now being called, to the notice of the powers that be in UFO investigation. R. L. Pearcy wrote thanking me for the statement regarding my UFO experience and enclosed two forms from BUFORA which he asked me to fill in and return. These would then be sent to their headquarters with my statement.

He mentioned that experiences like mine had been reported several times before in England over the years and many times in other parts of the world since 1945. This interested me and made me realise that others had obviously lost time too. Then he posed a theory. He wondered whether I had considered that the 'black darkness' could have been caused by the brilliant light suddenly going out and my eyes taking a while to adjust. This theory I discounted because I was already in darkness when the lights started to flash. He also suggested that I should ask the residents of the farm and the cottage if they had seen the lights or heard anything at the time, or whether they had seen me in my stationary car on the road outside their homes. This was something I hesitated to do as I was not sure how to handle it.

On 3rd December 1978 I answered the questions on the "UFO Sighting Account Forms" I had received.

- I filled in personal details and in answer to the question "Do you object to the publication of your name?" I answered, "No." I felt in no way afraid to talk about it, I did not think about ridicule or disbelief or that it would in any way be considered to be brave to do so. My main concern at that time was to find answers to my questions and reasons for this experience as quickly as possible.
- Then I drew my UFO but did not need to write an account as a copy was attached.
- I answered questions about the location of the sighting, the date, the time and for how long I observed the object. I placed 'A' on a curved line in a diagram to help indicate the altitude of the object above the horizon when I first noticed it and 'B' for its position when I last noticed it.
- I placed 'A' on the outside of a compass to indicate the direction in which I first observed the object and 'B' when I last saw it.
- I indicated the approximate height above ground level and answered that it did not disappear from view.
- I had not taken a photograph nor had I noticed any unusual effects on people, plants, etc. nearby. At the time of the sighting I was not aware that these points would be relevant to any enquiry.
- To "What was the main feature of the sighting which made you feel that the object was not natural or man-made?" I answered, "The brightness of the light, its shape and the fact that it was stationary."
- As I was alone I could give no names of other witnesses. A brief

description of the object was asked for under the headings of number, colour, sound, shape, sharply defined or hazy, and brightness compared to stars etc.

- The final question referred to the weather conditions at the time and I noted scattered cloud, a moderate wind, the odd star, a cold temperature and a dry day.

This is a very detailed examination which is given to each reported sighting and it helps BUFORA to file and collate similar reports. If anonymity is desired by the witness then this is all dealt with in the strictest confidence. That is a very important aspect of all investigations.

I realise now, though I didn't at the time, what BUFORA can do for everyone who sights something that is seemingly unidentifiable. Many things which members of the public do not understand about happenings in the air and sometimes on the ground may be thought to be UFOs, but BUFORA's team of trained investigators, through very thorough research, can find explanations for a large percentage of them.

Chapter Three

INVESTIGATION

The BUFORA organisation had now leapt into action. I remember feeling very impressed that the British UFO Research Association was involved and told myself that it must be a very unusual sighting for a group of such importance to be interested as I didn't think of it as being anything really special. Little did I know! The nearest investigators to Church Stowe at that time lived in Leicestershire. They had been put in touch with me too and a very thorough investigation was about to begin.

SEEN A UFO? The pamphlet asked – then UAPROL would like to hear about it.

'The Unidentified Aerial Phenomena Research Organisation of Leicester' had a twenty-four-hour Robophone Answering Service and those of us who had seen anything we could not explain were asked to make urgent contact, promised a strictly confidential questionnaire on request and no ridicule.

UAPROL was a non profit-making, non-political and non-religious organisation run by volunteers and its aims were to encourage and promote unbiased scientific investigation and research into Unidentified Flying Object Phenomena; to collect and disseminate evidence and data relating to Unidentified Flying Objects and to co-operate with persons and organisations engaged upon similar research. Membership was free, except for the stamped, self-addressed envelopes for the quarterly newsletters, and in February 1979 it was hoped there would shortly be a monthly news sheet.

Contact with the group was through Trevor Thornton who, with John Addison and Mark Brown, visited my home to investigate my sighting. They belonged to the Midlands UFO Network and they brought with them one of their daughters, a little girl of about nine or ten years old. I thought it rather strange at the time to involve someone so young. Little did I know that ten years later on my own ten-year-old granddaughter would become involved too after sighting two UFOs in Weedon.

The investigation involved the same questionnaire sent to me by R. L. Pearcy, but this time it meant much more as the investigators were able to ask for more detail in their questions and to link up my answers with the experiences of other witnesses, e.g. it was interesting to know that a dumb-bell shaped UFO had also been seen over Leicestershire during the daytime previous to my sighting and comparisons could be made, by the investigators, between the two.

After this, a visit to the area of the sighting was made and village people were also asked if they had seen anything at that particular time on that particular day. No-one in the village came forward on that occasion but much later I was to hear about a man and his wife who had seen a green and red light over Silverstone racetrack at 5.00 p.m. on that evening, of two people who had seen the lights over Weedon, and of a young man who had a strange and frightening experience not far away. He would not talk about this to anyone outside his family. Also there was a car whose engine cut out just outside the village at the same time as I was sitting in darkness with the lights flashing on the road in front of me. Not one of those people would come forward and help with the investigation then and I could not understand why. Astonished silence on hearing my story was by then turning to ridicule and for that reason I do understand their reaction. They did not want to become involved.

Following the investigation it was suggested again that I should contact the farmer and his family to see if they had noticed anything unusual at that time. This was not an easy thing to do, as I was not sure of their reaction, but the farmer's wife was interested, listened sympathetically and said she would mention it to her mother-in-law, on whose house and garden the brilliant circles of white light had shone. She was elderly and I thought that would be best as my details might have worried her. I was told later that she didn't believe a word of it and thought it to be hilarious, which pleased me as the last thing I wanted to do was to frighten anyone.

This had almost happened at another gathering when an elderly lady was listening. "I don't think I dare go home tonight," she had said and was obviously worried as she lived alone.

"Well, look at it this way," I said, "I was selected at lunch time when I

41

had the tightening sensation around my head, scanned on the way home when the car was stopped and rejected in the evening when I had the other tightening sensation around my head." Silence . . . "They obviously didn't need me," I added and this caused a laugh which relieved the tension and brought us all down to earth again. To this day I don't know what made me say that but I was to find, as the years went by, that it was probably very near to the truth.

Following my own questions to the villagers another reaction occurred when a visitor came to see my husband one evening. When I opened the door this man looked at me, burst out laughing and said, "I don't believe a word of it." He roared with controllable laughter punctuating it with the same words – "I don't believe a word of it!"

I had been washing up the tea things when he rang the doorbell and as I stood there drying my hands on the tea towel, the only thought which came into my mind was, "What on earth is the silly man talking about?" I stood there calmly looking at him knowing that at some time he was bound to run out of steam – then the penny dropped. He was referring to my UFO, the last thing that had been on my mind as I stood at the kitchen sink. As expected in time he did stop. Perhaps his outburst was not having the desired effect on me? "Well," I said, as soon as the opportunity arose, "think about it like this. When they invade the earth, and I see no reason why they should not be able to do so, as soon as they get to Church Stowe they'll either choose me as their leader, or I'll be the first one they'll exterminate. Either way I'll have nothing to worry about – but you will."

I have often wondered what made me say that too.

Following the investigation the Leicester group's UAPROL newsletter carried an account of my sighting written by W. A. Hayes and ending with diagrams showing the position of the car within the village when it had stopped, a diagram of the UFO and a map of the roads in relation to the incident.

Then following this was a final paragraph relating how another incident had been reported from Northampton that same evening. It would appear that four ladies had left Byfield at 7.20 p.m. to travel via Woodford Halse to Northampton. During the journey they had seen a parallel beam of light shoot out of the clouds in the direction of Church Stowe. Later a green and a red light were seen and these paced the car for a while. The car engine also faltered for no apparent reason. A full report was promised in the next newsletter.

That was the first I'd heard of the sighting and I waited eagerly to read the full account.

* * *

A full page of detailed maps headed 'Simplified Map of Area of Sightings with Apparent Electro-Magnetic Effects, Northamptonshire 22 November 1978' accompanied the accounts of the two sightings in the next issue of the UAPROL newsletter.

It was thought that my UFO, or a similar one, had put in an appearance just two hours after my encounter. As those four ladies were approaching Preston Capes in their car at about 7.30 p.m. they turned a bend in the road and a short parallel-sided beam of light shot out of the clouds. About three seconds later this was repeated, the beams being projected towards Church Stowe.

Turning right onto the Preston Capes road they saw two lights, one red and one green, the red one on the left and the green on the right, as had been those that I had seen over the A5.

In the account it was reported that the lights were at an angular elevation of about 45°, they appeared to be 12 inches apart at arm's length and the object crossed the road in front of the car just before it arrived at Preston Capes. Estimations with these figures showed that the object must have been quite close to the car, perhaps within a quarter of a mile and it proceeded to pace the car on the right-hand side of the road as far as Little Preston where the green and red lights changed to a single white one which switched off abruptly. There was no noise from the object but while the car was being paced the engine faltered, forcing the driver to change from top to third gear. She reported that the whole encounter lasted about three minutes during which time she felt a sense of 'foreboding'.

The investigators who visited me studied this case also and concluded that though they could not say for certain it was the same object in both cases, it did seem very likely.

Here also was an excellent example of how the close questioning of witnesses by trained investigators using, e.g. the angular elevation of the lights and the distance they appeared to be at arm's length, could produce fairly accurate measurements which would be useful in their research.

The report ended by asking – "Was it a co-incidence that the primary witnesses in both cases were married women travelling by car in the night-time countryside? Remember what had happened to Mrs. Oakensen, what would have happened to Mrs. "X" had she been driving alone? One cannot help but wonder . . . "

"Sounds quite mysterious and very intriguing," I innocently remarked to John. "Sounds as if they know something I don't."

"I shouldn't worry about it," he comfortingly replied. So I didn't.

* * *

In Church Stowe and at work my sighting had been a nine-day wonder and I had found no answers to any of my questions. I assumed that one day I might do so, but I was not very confident about that so I put it all behind me and decided to pretend it had never happened. It would be wrong to say it never surfaced in my thoughts. It did. But, like so many other people I went through a period when I did not want to talk about it and I stopped joining in conversations where UFOs were mentioned. I told myself that when I did mention having seen a UFO people usually wanted to hear all the details and it took such a long time to tell. Anyway, most of the people I was with had heard it all before and I told myself they would be bored.

So I tried to carry on as normal, at the same time trying to behave as if nothing had happened to change me in any way, though looking back, I do remember one occasion when I was driving along the back roads from Weedon to Church Stowe after an evening course at the Teachers' Centre. Suddenly a very bright light was switched on in the distance. My heart jumped into my mouth and I was conscious of saying out loud, "Oh no, not again. *Please!*"

But the panic soon abated when I realised it could have been someone in Farthingstone village switching on an outside light at his home. It was very bright and had made me realise that however calm I might have been on the day of that encounter, lack of understanding of it had really made me quite worried inwardly, and I now needed time to adjust before I could cope with the reasons for those strange experiences.

Chapter Four

HYPNOSIS

Whatever I had thought before, it soon became obvious that interest in my sighting had not died down nor had my mind stopped trying to find the reason for it.

I travelled that route almost every evening on my way home from work and each time I expected to see those lights as I turned on to the A5. The missing time was referred to as a 'time lapse' and I still did not understand the lack of light in the village on that particular day. It had seemed only seconds as I sat and watched the lights flash around the car, but about fifteen minutes of time must have elapsed during that period.

The following day, the same journey had taken me only fifteen minutes instead of the thirty minutes on the previous day and on rounding the corner where the lights had flashed, my own headlights lit up the road, the houses and the farm buildings, and everywhere seemed light although I was arriving in the village at a later time in the day. It was nowhere near as dark then at that spot, nor has it been since. Incidentally the faulty sidelight bulb in my car, which was not working when I left the Teachers' Centre the day before, functioned normally afterwards and never did need replacing.

Over ten years later it was suggested to me that the reason for the darkness and the flashing lights may have been to take my mind off something else which was happening at the time, and which I was not destined to realise the significance of until much later.

Although I had feelings along those lines at the time, they were not as organised as that suggestion and it came as quite a surprise when on 23rd April 1979 I received a phone call from Martin Keatman, a Regional Investigations Co-ordinator for BUFORA, who wished to discuss my experience and to ask if I would be willing to be hypnotised in order that I might possibly recall some of the things which had happened during the time lapse.

I had a feeling of apprehension regarding the unknown. I had never been hypnotised before and had only heard tales of ridiculous antics performed by people who succumbed. However, I was aware that Graham Phillips was a qualified psychoanalyst and hypnotherapist and that Martin and Andrew Collins would be present. It was to be my own decision and I was asked to think about it and let him know how I felt.

I discussed this with John and we decided that we would go ahead with it on one condition, and that was that he should be present. So a convenient time for all was arranged. I was to be hypnotised on 18th August 1979 almost nine months after the sighting and on my 28th wedding anniversary, one which I shall never forget.

I spent the morning of that day preparing a buffet tea and tidying the house for their visit after lunch. Their arrival gave me the first shock of the day. They all looked so young. It is said that when policemen appear to be young you are really getting old, well that was exactly how I felt when they arrived. They seemed to be about the same age as our sons and so knowledgeable about UFOs. I had no interest at all in them until that strange journey home nine months before. They were really interesting to talk to and amazed that I had read no books at all on the subject.

It was explained to me that I was to be psychoanalysed first to see if I would be a suitable subject for hypnosis. As I remember, that consisted of a number of questions only one of which I recall. It was this – If you were walking through a wood and came across a tree which had fallen across your path, which end would you walk round to continue your journey? Having lived during my childhood in a village near a wood and spent many happy hours playing there, it was a situation I had met before. So I answered that it would all depend on the thickness of the trunk across the path and that knowing me (a very agile person) I would probably climb over the top of it and continue on my way. I recall an immediate bewildered look, then laughter. I then explained that in my opinion there were so many things to take into consideration like the size of the roots and branches of the tree, also the weather because if it were wet there could be mud to contend with, and how long the tree had been in that position as the trunk may have been unsafe, so that, in my opinion, a simple answer could not be expected. I have realised since that

I never did find out if my answer was the right one, or in fact whether there really was a correct one.

However Graham seemed to be satisfied with my answers and it was decided that I should be hypnotised. I understood that nothing might come from it, but perhaps something would; that I would be under a slight hypnotic regression and that I would remember everything afterwards, also that in the following days more may come into my mind, then things would become clearer.

Tape recorders were set at the ready, including ours, as I was determined that no-one was going away knowing something about the encounter that I did not know myself. We were all prepared to listen to the results at a more relaxing time.

The hypnosis was of a slightly regressive kind. I remember Graham counting and being told to hold my right arm up in front of me at right angles to my body. I could hear what was going on in the room, the clock ticking and the change-over of cassettes. It seemed to me that I was getting nowhere and I remember telling myself that it was not working.

Suddenly there it was again, a tightening sensation around my head just as I had had on the two previous occasions at lunch time and in the evening on the day of my encounter. A large circle of brilliant white light came towards me until I could see only the top of it and circles of equally brilliant white light pulsated out from it. I got hotter and hotter and my head hurt. I was sweating and very frightened. My arms shook. I was sure I was in a sitting position as I could feel no weight on my legs.

The light and the pulsating circles of light, all with clearly defined edges and no fuzziness, receded into the distance until there was just a very small circle of white light very similar to that of the torch used by an optician to inspect a patient's eye during an examination.

Then with the small light still in the distance, a long thin shape appeared between it and me and to the left of the light. It was rather ghost-like, with a head and body and very smooth edged. It was grey in colour with a silvery outline, possibly caused by the effect of the light behind it. It appeared to come really close to me, then to go away into the darkness, but it did not change size. Then it was no longer there.

Almost immediately another shape, this time more rectangular but with smooth corners instead of angular ones, appeared to the right of the light. It stood on one of its rounded corners.

This was also grey with a silvery outline and behaved in exactly the same way as the first one. They did not get progressively smaller. At that point they were simply no longer there.

Then as I watched the small light still shining in the distance they reappeared together, seemed to come up to me and then go away. As suddenly as they had appeared they had gone again. The light went out. I was shaking and extremely hot. My head hurt even more – and I was absolutely terrified.

It was at this point that I was brought out of the hypnosis. My headache was relieved by autosuggestion. My body gradually cooled down and I was extremely glad it was all over.

Graham Phillips said that over the next few days more memories might come into my mind and suggested I should make a note of anything else I remembered and let him know. Another session would be required for full recall and arrangements could be made as and when I felt it to be the right time.

We had a relaxed meal and discussed what had occurred. Before they left, about three hours after they had arrived, they showed me Vol. 1 No. 1 of the *Strange Phenomena* monthly magazine which cost 75p. The Editor was Graham S. Phillips and the Senior Research Co-ordinator, Andy Collins.

Although they had been surprised when they arrived that I had never read any books about UFOs, now came the time for them to say that it was not wise for me to do so yet. I had been offered a copy of their magazine, but on inspection they found the contents to be either too similar to my own experience or to be about subjects it was not advisable for me to know about at that time. Gradually, much to everyone's amusement, articles were removed and I was eventually given the cover of the magazine. This has a special place in the scrapbook I have kept over the years. It was not to be until much later that I learned the reason for what, at the time, I thought to be this eccentric behaviour.

Eleven years afterwards and still not having read any books on the subject I heard the word 'contamination' in connection with hypnosis – and then I understood. Had I read anything at all about UFOs my mind might have retained that information and it could then have come through the next hypnosis session as being a genuine part of my own experience.

Later that evening John and I went out for an anniversary dinner. He'd been interested in the session and said that I had sat with my arm up for forty minutes. He wanted to talk about the happenings of that afternoon but the effect on me was such that my mind was all 'mixed up' with incredulous thoughts which I could not get into perspective, and I am afraid that I was far from good company.

The following days I spent in a state of disbelief. This was something I felt I had to get organised by myself so I involved no-one in the family or at work. It had to be put into some kind of order and I felt that I had to have a reason for it all.

Three days later I woke up feeling that in some way I could cope with it so I wrote a report for Graham, with the drawings of the 'beings', as I decided to call them, and diagrams of the light at its various stages. Immediately following the hypnosis I could not have coped with another session. There was too much new information (which was alien to my understanding) for my mind to deal with and it took me a very long time to come to terms with it all.

For many months I did not tell anyone about that day mainly because I did not know what to think about it myself. The answers for which I had hoped had not been forthcoming. Instead I had more questions. The tightening sensation around my head seemed to link it all together but –

- Why did the bright circle of light come towards me? What was it doing?
- What was the purpose of those circles of light which pulsated outwards from it?
- What were those ghost-like shapes? Why did they come and go? Were they observing me for some reason?
- If so, what was that reason? And –
- Why was I terrified at this point when on the day I had been so perfectly calm?

There was so much to sort out and I felt that this was something which I could only do by myself.

Chapter Five

A WIDER VIEWPOINT

The local newspaper reporters kept up a lively interest in my sighting and whenever we met they asked if anything else had happened. As we worked closely with them from the Teachers' Centre, it seemed natural to say that I had been asked by John Barden, then Vice-Chairman of UAPROL, to accompany him on a phone-in programme on Radio Leicester on Tuesday, March 18th 1980.

I was given permission for the morning's absence by my Senior Education Inspector and I think 'bemused' would sum up his feelings regarding the exercise. Many people who had by then become interested in UFOs were going to listen in and my husband took the radio to work with him. It seemed amazing to me that so many people were still interested. There had been nothing in the newspapers at all about it since just after it had happened almost eighteen months before.

I arrived in good time at the Radio Leicester building, met John Barden and together we waited until just before the programme was due to start, then we were ushered into the studio where Morgan Cross was to present it. I have always been one to enjoy a 'new experience' and there I was for the first time in a BBC Radio Studio and about to go on the air.

Although it was exciting, I was worried about what might be expected of me. All I knew about UFOs was from one personal experience. If I am honest it was only my sighting in which I was interested. I still had read no books about UFOs or science fiction and if it were going to be required of me to make comparisons with, or to discuss other people's experiences, there was no way in which I felt competent to do so.

I had not met John Barden before, but when I spoke to him on the phone prior to this meeting, I had the feeling that the part I was to play was to just tell my story. I was happy about that, and hopefully it would be a bonus to learn something about UFOs during the programme and come away a little wiser.

Before I had time to feel nervous I heard Morgan Cross introducing the programme. "Well, in just a moment or two," he announced, "I'll be talking to John Barden and Elsie Oakensen about Unidentified Flying Objects. If you think you've seen one, give us a call. Certainly Elsie Oakensen has seen one and I have a rather frightening document all about it in front of me – but we'll find out more about that in just a moment."

A record was played, then I was introduced by Morgan giving a partial account of my sighting. ". . . with her nose pressed to the windscreen and absolutely fascinated by it, she drove directly under it." John Barden and I were introduced to the listeners and I was then asked to continue the story.

I was on the air. Thousands of people were listening. Radio Leicester was our local radio too. It was to be some years before Radio Northampton was born. I related the rest of the details of my encounter, punctuated by questions from Morgan and then it was John's turn to take part in the programme.

He was complimented on the depth of the investigation into my sighting and asked if it was a typical report. Here I was to learn that it was not. He said that this was an "exceptional case of its kind". Apparently sightings were normally of lights flying through the sky with no obvious detail, but because of the effects on the car, mine could be compared to the film *Close Encounters of the Third Kind* where cars had come to a halt. The influence of such films on people was discussed but John Barden told him that I had described what I saw quite clearly and that from the investigations they had carried out at the time of the sighting, they could find no reason to disbelieve me.

They discussed the 'very well documented' maps which accompanied the report in the UAPROL newsletter and I was to learn that the 'electro-magnetic effects' referred to an interference of the electrical system of the car by some sort of magnetic disturbance. During the programme there were about a dozen callers describing their own sightings of UFOs, most coming under the heading of "Low Definition Sightings". There was a lady who saw the same object regularly and which John Barden promised to look into. Another saw an enormous orangey light and described it as "quite an experience". This prompted questions to me about my feelings at the time of my close encounter. Was I worried? Was I frightened?

"Not at all," I confidently replied, "it was *surprise* when I got to Weedon, surprise that the red and green lights did not move and were attached to a stationary object. *Curosity* when the circular lights started to flash on and off and I wanted to know more about them, where they came from and why they were flashing. No, I was not frightened. I had no sense of fear at all, just absolute *amazement*."

The evening sighting by the four ladies at Preston Capes was mentioned and John Barden was asked if he knew what those objects were doing and what the organisation thought they could possibly be. He said that with the information which was available at that time it was impossible to say what UFOs definitely were but the favourite theory was that they were visitors from another planet. However we had nothing to prove that, or disprove it.

It was explained that UFO investigators worked very closely with all authorities to check whether a sighting could be an aircraft or a piece of space debris. The latter was described as little starlike objects which move through the sky at a steady pace in one direction and if they happen to be spinning they will twinkle. My red and green lights could have been taken for an aircraft coming in to land, in fact that was my first thought, but apparently not in the way I had reported it. The question of a government cover-up was raised and surprise expressed that with the type of radar equipment available at the time these objects did not show up on it. It was later pointed out that the sky is literally full of unidentified flying objects, most of which have a purely rational explanation.

Apparently the fact that sometimes only one person sees something which others around do not see is not unusual. There have been cases where a very spectacular object was seen close to by only two or three witnesses. Then, on the other hand, two hundred witnesses had seen something resembling a Vulcan bomber, but with absolutely no sound and as it had passed over the houses of people who had pets it was found that the animals had become frightened and tried to hide. This is a common occurrence when they are in the vicinity of a UFO. Sometimes witnesses will also report a strange smell.

Another caller spoke of a sighting which she and her family had experienced whilst on holiday in America and she expressed her surprise at reading an account of it in her local newspaper some time after her return. It reminded me that I had sent an account of my close encounter to a friend in America soon after it happened and he had written to say that he had passed it to the appropriate authority there.

One lady caller told how her husband had seen two men walking along a street one morning. They had silver faces, were dressed in silver and wore helmets like a diver's. This prompted a discussion on extra-terrestrials. There is no evidence to prove that 'people' from another planet do visit us on Earth, but if they do one theory would be that they are extraterrestrials. Another is that they are time-travellers or come from another dimension, but as yet there is no proof.

What did I think? Well I had no proof to offer, but I had not explained at the beginning of the programme that my journey home that night had taken fifteen minutes longer than it usually did and I assumed that the time was spent in the car whilst the lights were flashing around it. Is it possible that something like that may have been happening. There might have been 'somebody' walking around the car. I didn't know. I was not conscious of seeing anything at that particular time.

Pressed as to whether I would be prepared to believe it, I said that I thought I would, then explained that I had never seen the film *Close Encounters of the Third Kind* nor had I read any books on that or any related subject. My own knowledge of this was only through my own experience. I had probably been very sceptical before the encounter, certainly I never gave the subject any thought but now I did believe there was something. We are a small planet within an enormous solar system and it seems logical to me that we are not the only people within the universe. I can believe that there would be inhabitants on other planets. Had I not suggested a possible invasion of the earth to a caller at my home when he ridiculed me soon after it had happened?

It was also assumed that if these 'visitors' could fly in this way and travel millions of miles to get here and if they were in a humanoid form, then they would come in peace. Technically, to be able to travel so far they would be much more advanced than we are and so perhaps they would have passed through the stages of atom bombs etc., realised how ridiculous war is and found more efficient and more effective ways to solve their problems. A caller toward the end of the programme said he felt there was no evidence to support the theory that an older civilization would necessarily be technically superior to ours.

Everyone who rang in and had seen a UFO had started with an open mind but now definitely believed in them, though no-one understood what they were, where they came from, or why they came. One man still remembered details of the one he had seen twenty-three years before.

Morgan Cross summed up the programme by saying what a fascinating subject it was to talk about, mainly because some people believe whilst others don't and he said that he was sure we would find out more about UFOs in the years to come. I found myself agreeing with him. This was the first time I had been involved in UFOs from a wider viewpoint and I had to admit it did fascinate me.

After that programme I realised that at no point during it did I mention my session of hypnosis, not even when I was given a direct opportunity to do so. I had found it so traumatic and so hard to understand that my mind had shut it out completely. The time was obviously not right yet to publicise it as I felt unable to give logical answers to the many questions I was sure I would be asked. I had had my first experience of broadcasting on the radio, one which I was to find would stand me in good stead for the future.

My own encounter had been discussed openly and frankly in considerable detail. I had learned so many things about UFOs that day and what a vast range of knowledge could be gathered from a study of such a phenomenon.

* * *

The new Editor of the *Daventry Weekly Express* at that time was Keith Ridley and he was as interested in UFOs as Peter. He had also heard about the phone-in programme.

On Friday 21st March I was featured on the front page. 'UFO Hypnosis Probe to find "lost time"' the headline read. He had asked me outright if I had considered hypnosis. How could I say no? But I did not tell him all the details, only about the tightening sensation around my head and how I was able to link it with the others I'd had on the day. I said I was expecting to have another session soon and would keep him informed. This was quite true.

But there was one thing that I did not expect and that was to be the hottest piece of news that week. It was a surprise to see myself smiling away on the front page, but more of a shock to see the editorial inside. It was headed 'Brave Lady' and to do it justice I print it in full with the kind permission of the present Editor, Peter Aengenheister.

Viewpoint . . . Daventry Weekly Express . . . Brave Lady
Mrs. Elsie Oakensen, head of Daventry Teachers' Centre, is
a very brave lady indeed.

On Tuesday, Mrs. Oakensen took part in a radio phone-in programme to tell listeners about the night she believes she saw an unidentified flying object.

Afterwards we spoke to Mrs. Oakensen and she told us quite openly about her hypnosis sessions to try to discover what actually happened to her that night.

Yes, it does sound like an extract from a science-fiction novel, but anyone who knows Mrs. Oakensen will tell you she is anything but a crank.

And she had a great deal to lose by telling her story in the first place and taking part in Tuesday's phone-in programme for Radio Leicester.

If there is a reasonable explanation for her experiences we feel sure that Mrs. Oakensen would be happy to know about it. However sceptical people may be, they should remember one thing – it would have been much easier for her never to have mentioned a thing outside her own home.

That piece of support was wonderful and it gave me the courage I needed to talk about it much more openly. Many of the people who read the paper asked me to keep them in touch with future happenings and through it I met many with a genuine interest in UFOs.

Chapter Six

THE PHONE CALL THAT CHANGED MY LIFE

During the years that followed much happened. I continued with my work and developed new interests. Life became very hectic. I rarely thought of that day in November 1978 and when I did hear UFOs mentioned in a conversation, I did not join in. I tried to behave as if it had never happened and was quite sure that I was very successfully doing so.

At the end of April 1983, because of my increasing back problems, I had been advised to take early retirement from my post at the Teachers' Centre. I was going through a very painful period and was losing all confidence in myself.

Richard Coffey was a very caring new doctor who had taken over the Weedon practice. He had heaps of time for his patients and his main concern for me was that in retirement I should not vegetate, so much excellent advice came my way. John and I had taken up ballroom dancing seriously a few years before and had completed each year with an examination at the relevant level, despite increasing pain from the arthritis which was now also in my feet and knees.

"Carry on dancing," Dr. Coffey had said. "Dancing is a very good exercise for the spine and exercise is good for you, even if it hurts. You must keep your muscles tight. The body's own corset is much better than those you buy in the shops." It was that advice that I continually reminded myself of when I was depressed and which I have quoted to many others since.

Thursday night was one of our dancing nights. We belonged to the Potterspury School of Dancing and travelled the twelve or so miles from Church Stowe three times a week, once for our own class and two evenings, including Thursdays, to partner pupils in their classes at lower levels. For some reason, probably because the Women's Institute needed the hall that night, there was no class on Thursday, 6th August 1987. We were having a leisurely evening at home when just after 8.00 p.m. the phone rang and I answered it. The caller said her name was Jenny Randles.

Hers was a name which, with an address, I had written down following an interview which I had heard on one of Radio 4's Woman's Hour programmes. That was during the period when I was on sick leave from the Centre prior to my enforced retirement. Jenny had asked listeners to write to her if they had seen anything they could not identify and I had every intention of doing just that, but like so many other things at that time I never got around to it. I had not heard the introduction to the programme so was not aware of her role as Director of Investigations for BUFORA. Had I done so I would, of course, have known that she already had access to my case.

That night on the telephone Jenny asked me if I could remember what happened on 22nd November 1978. How could I forget? though Heaven knows I had tried hard enough to do so. Since the hypnosis in April of the following year and the Radio Leicester phone-in programme which were followed by the newspaper report, I had put the whole episode into the background and now, without warning, I was asked to recount the whole experience.

Jenny told me she was writing a book and wanted to include an account of my close encounter in it. She was doing some research for BUFORA, working in conjunction with Dr. John Shaw of Manchester University, and was contacting anyone who had had an experience like mine in the last thirty years. I agreed to send newspaper cuttings and my own report on the hypnosis. She said she would arrange a further session if I agreed. So I consulted John and he agreed that if she thought it would be of some use then it should be arranged. My previous session, although it had been taped, had not had very satisfactory results. It seemed to have been a good thing that there had only been a slight regression so that I was able to write an account of it and the subsequent memories recalled in the days following the session.

After writing a letter to Jenny enclosing newspaper reports and the account I had written, I received a letter back stating that she was having second thoughts about hypnosis being the right answer, and asking me if I would do an experiment for her.

This was it. At some time when I had a free half hour or so I was to relax somewhere comfortable and try to picture the experience as it had happened, to tell myself that I was writing a story and imagine in detail what would happen next. I was not to overdo it, but to note anything that came into my mind, then record it on paper or tape.

Jenny had tried this with other people who had had an experience like mine, but obviously told me no details as it would have influenced the experiment. She described it as a way of tapping into my subconscious mind, but I like to think of it as a kind of self-hypnosis.

The book Jenny was writing, called *Abduction*, was to be about hypnosis and cases like mine. It would be a revolutionary new book and I felt very proud that I had been asked to help with this controversial new study, which was to be published in Spring 1988. It would represent a new step forward in the research into UFOs and was to include accounts from people in countries world-wide who had experienced loss of time and who, during it, believed they had come into contact with unidentifiable entities. It was hoped that psychologists would be interested enough to offer their help and a tentative hope was that through this, someone locally might offer to help me unravel the mystery of my missing fifteen minutes.

Jenny was also in agreement that I should inform my local newspaper. Peter Aengenheister had recently asked if anything was happening. He had 'gone up' in the journalistic world and was now the Editor of the *Daventry Weekly Express*. He had always asked me to keep him informed.

On September 10th 1987 the page 5 headline read: 'Nine Years after UFO Sighting – Close Encounters Relived Once More.' An article written by Susan Ward impressed me immensely. She had spoken to Jenny and, as I was still in a state of shock and excitement about the sudden renewal of interest and the prospect of being featured in a book, it all became much clearer when I read the article.

My sighting was described as being on the 'fringe of credibility' and as a 'Close Encounter of the Fourth Kind' – A description which I was to learn meant I was one of a group of people world-wide who also claimed to have had experience of direct contact (and some with on-board contact) with what I had always affectionately called 'those beings'.

I began to realise that there really must be something unusual about my encounter. I had heard of 'Close Encounters of the Third Kind', though at that point I had not seen the film, but my close encounter was of the *fourth* kind. I had been 'abducted' This was the first time my 'time lapse' had been so described to me.

Jenny had told Susan that my experience had been particularly interesting because of the sighting that same evening by the four ladies at Preston Capes. Apparently it was an unusual feature in close encounter cases but it had corroborated my sighting and in that way had made it somewhat 'special'.

I looked up at the sky for the photograph which accompanied the article, shielding my eyes from the sun with my hand, as Peter Spencer snapped away. 'Elsie still scanning the skies' the caption read. It was a very good report and caused comment wherever I went. Interest was renewed and I found myself talking about it again. Now, perhaps, I would begin to find answers to some of my questions.

To do Jenny's experiment was easier said than done! Each time I settled down during the day the phone rang, or someone came to the door. At night time it was no easier. I had not realised how many noises there were in the stillness of the night. Then a week later, just as if it were all planned, Nick Herbert, a presenter for BBC Radio Northampton, rang and suggested an exercise which was to have very far-reaching implications.

He said he had read the article in the *Daventry Weekly Express* and that he would like to cover it on radio. Could he come and interview me the following day? He arrived at the arranged time and sat and listened to my account of that strange experience.

"How do you feel about going over the area and talking me through it?" he asked suddenly. "We could stop at each point where something happened and it would help me to visualise it better."

So, off we set for the lay-by on the A5 near which the UFO had been and where on this occasion we were able to stop, but on that day nearly nine years before, although feeling compelled to do so, I had not felt it would be wise because of the amount of traffic on the road at that time and for fear of causing an accident.

The traffic rushed by as I described the UFO and he asked searching questions which forced me to remember details which I had put to the back of my mind. "We have a grey shape over the road and a big ball or circle on each end, so how big was the whole object? You just drove straight under this? How long did it take you to go under it? Was it a few seconds or longer?"

Well, I couldn't say. I had just travelled at the same speed as the other traffic on the road at that time.

Then we moved to the top of Stowe Hill just off the A5. "So, you've left the main road and have turned right towards Church Stowe. We are at a slight brow of a hill. Now what happened here and what did you do?" he asked. It was here that I had stopped to look back and had noticed that the object was still in the same place over the A5 and that I was about level with it. Then, as I looked, the green light had started to flash.

Reaching the third part of the journey, by turning right at the 'T' junction into the village, I explained how, although my car was in third gear and the accelerator pedal was flat on the floor of the car, it was slowing down and had almost come to a stop. But there was no panic on my part, only unkind thoughts about the mechanic who had serviced the car that day! At this point I had forgotten that dumb-bell shaped object under which I had driven not so long before and when the car had started normally after putting it into first gear I was happy enough to continue my journey home.

So, under the trees we drove and at the end of them I explained that it was at that point where I was last conscious of being in control of my car. Then we drove round a right-angled bend to the farm gate where I had found myself to be sitting in the car but in complete darkness whilst the brilliant white circles of light had flashed on to the ground around the front of it (in semicircles to the right, left and right again until the last one was turned, shone up the front of the cottage and off the top). Then, after a few seconds sitting in darkness the natural light returned and I found myself about thirty yards further down the road, in third gear, driving normally again.

I said that I had no idea what had caused all this and he asked if it were just as if it had been a dream. I explained about what I then called the tightening 'bands' around my head at lunch time and later in the evening and he suggested "sensations", which I thought to be a better description. I told him about the fifteen minutes' 'time lapse' and the hypnosis I had undergone in an attempt to find out what had happened during that time.

His last question was, "Is there any way you can explain what happened that day?"

"I can't," was my short answer, but I knew then that in no way would I give up. I felt there was an answer somewhere.

That outing was really exciting and in bed that night I found myself going over the whole thing. I noticed no interruptions. All noises seemed blocked out and I suddenly realised that conditions were right to do Jenny's experiment. Nick's questions had made me think deeper about each happening so that my mind had become receptive to investigation and as I lay there thoughts came flooding in. At 1.00 a.m. I got up and wrote everything down.

Later that morning I listened to the Radio Northampton broadcast. It was presented in sections over a period of thirty minutes, punctuated with what Nick had decided was appropriate music. Not being musical myself I cannot comment on the choice but general opinion following the broadcast pronounced it an ideal selection.

Afterwards I put my notes into some kind of order, but not into story form. I could not be sure that they would be an accurate account of what had happened and I felt uneasy believing that to find answers to my questions would be such a simple task. It was not yet the right time for me to be quoted as saying "This is what actually happened." So I listed the possibilities. They all seemed reasonable to me and I began to wonder if any of them would eventually prove to be true. The one thing I needed was proof. This was only the beginning, a start towards finding if it were at all possible.

Chapter Seven

THE EXPERIMENT

I had already written to Jenny saying that I was having difficulty finding the right conditions in which to do the experiment, but that as I don't give up easily I was sure that I would soon get a result. I just hoped that it would not be too late as the book was due to be published about six months from that time. So it was with much relief that I was able to complete the exercise and send to her the following possibilities:

- Perhaps the hypnosis session was at the beginning of the darkest time as the hypnotherapist had said, although I always felt it coincided with the first interference of the car engine.
- I wonder if the brilliant white light which came towards me under hypnosis was what had met me as I came out from under the line of trees after the car engine had first stopped, but under which I travelled after it had started again? I also wondered if the grey and silver figures which I saw were the "beings" who manned the UFO and whether it was they who had caused my car to finally stop about fifty yards further on from the end of the trees and round a right-angled bend in the road along which I do not recall travelling?
- During hypnosis I was conscious of being in a sitting position. During the 'blackness' session I was definitely sitting behind the steering wheel of my car. I could see the shape of the car bonnet, the road, the farm gateway, the house and the frame of the windscreen as the lights shone.
- The car must have come to a halt on the wrong side of the road because the circle of light on the left of my car was definitely on the road whilst the one on my right was in the garden of the cottage.
- I wonder if something came down from the UFO and enveloped the

car and the area immediately around it? The complete darkness could have been caused by a kind of curtain or barrier dropping down to ground level from the UFO and excluding all daylight.

- Could the enveloping darkness have been from the end of the tree-covered part of the road (which I remember driving to, and was in third gear) to the gate of the Old Rectory, where I became conscious of driving again (also in third gear)?
- Could that entire corner have been in darkness for that time? I could only see the cottage as the last brilliant white light shone on to it and I could not see the farmhouse which was in front of me and to my left-hand side.
- I had spoken to the farmer's wife a few days later. She and her family were not in the village at that time. The occupants of the other houses were not aware that anything had happened so close to their homes. Could these people have been made to be unaware of the presence of the UFO by its occupants?
- I am sure I was not taken into the UFO because the circular lights lit up the farm gate, the road around my car and the garden of the cottage to my right as I sat in the driving seat.
- As there were no beams, the lights must have been very close, perhaps immediately above me.
- Perhaps those shapes I saw under hypnosis were still around the car as the lights shone? Perhaps the brilliant light I saw under hypnosis was the same light which, instead of shining toward me and pulsating outwards in semicircles, now shone downwards from above my car level?
- The last circle of light shone on the cottage garden, then it went up the wall at the front of the house as if turned at that angle by someone holding a torch.
- I had time to say, "Good Gracious", then normal light and visibility returned and I was conscious of being about thirty yards further along the road, driving normally in third gear.
- Could this (and perhaps more) have happened in the time which cannot be accounted for?
- With the tightening bands around my head at 1.30 p.m., under hypnosis at approximately 5.30 p.m. and again after 7.00 p.m. (this one perhaps coinciding with the Byfield ladies' description of 'short, parallel beams of light which shot out of the clouds projected towards Church Stowe. This phenomenon was repeated some three seconds

later . . .' – Midlands UFO report by W. A. Haynes), I am now convinced that what I said jokingly after the experience, that I was "selected at 1.30 p.m., scanned at 5.30 p.m. and rejected after 7.00 p.m.", really could be true.

I sent these observations to Jenny by recorded delivery so that they were not lost in the post and offered any further help that I could. She thanked me for my help and confirmed that her book, entitled *Abduction*, was to be published in April 1988.

On the 3rd of November there came another surprise call. "How did I feel about appearing on television?" Very shocked and apprehensive but pleasantly surprised to be honest. I hoped it would not turn out like the offer I had received in the summer of the previous year.

I had been having my hair shampooed when a customer who came into the hairdresser's told me that the presenters of ITV's 'Central Weekend' programme were asking for people with an interest in UFOs to contact them. They were preparing a programme on that subject at a later date. She knew that I fitted this description and asked me to send details of my encounter.

My health was still poor at the time but I did send copies of my reports on the sighting and hypnosis and heard nothing until I received a letter dated 2nd September 1986 telling me that Central TV was transmitting a live 'Central Weekend' programme on UFOs on Friday September 5th and inviting me, plus a friend, to sit in the audience.

The letter actually arrived on Thursday the 4th and although the prospect of appearing on television was a welcome one I felt there was no way that I, in my state of health, could even consider a journey to Birmingham during the following evening, then somehow try to complete a return journey via Coventry, Rugby and Northampton in the early hours of Saturday morning, so I watched it from home instead.

The subject was covered in about twenty-five minutes of the programme and not as fully as I would have hoped. Had I made the journey to attend I would not have felt happy at the inconvenience I would have had for such a short time. The staff at the hairdresser's and the lady who suggested I made contact were most apologetic when next I saw them. They had been disappointed too.

But this time it would be different. Robert Kilroy-Silk was doing a series of 'Kilroy' programmes from 9.20-10.00 a.m. each weekday and he had planned to do one about UFOs. Jenny had put my name forward and the programme was expected to be recorded live at Lime Grove TV Studios in London on the following Wednesday afternoon. She named a contact who would ring me the following day for a chat but I soon came down to earth again as the call did not come when expected. Later, I learned that 'Kilroy', being a current affairs programme, used topical subjects as they cropped up, but occasionally need a 'slot-in' programme and that was what the UFO one was to be.

I decided then that I had better watch one or two programmes to see what the format was so that I would have some idea what to expect when I was contacted. The following week all was set for my visit. I was asked to be at the television studio by 2.00 p.m. for the recording of the programme which would be shown the following morning.

I had several conversations with the programme researcher during the few days prior to the recording and a great deal of time was spent in going over my account of the sighting so that he understood every word. 'Kilroy' was a discussion programme which included experts on this chosen subject, people who had had sightings of UFOs, others who had expressed an interest in them, and some disbelievers too. The programme would be roughly divided into four sections. The first would involve the people who had seen unidentifiable objects and lights, followed by a discussion on this. The third part was where I would be expected to contribute. Then finally they would come to the non-believers and sceptics who would be voicing their opinions.

On Tuesday 14th November 1978 I arrived at Euston Station allowing myself plenty of time to relax before taking a taxi to Lime Grove Studios in order to arrive by 2.00 p.m. I was wearing my red suit with a navy and white striped blouse and navy shoes. I sat on a seat at the station watching the people pass and thinking about another new experience for me – my television debut. I did hope that when I was asked to speak I would not forget what I had come all that way to tell the viewers. Suddenly I was awakened sharply from my daydreams.

"I know you," said a cheerful Irish voice, "you're an actress you are. You're on the television in that programme on Monday and Wednesday evenings. I know, 'Coronation Street'. You're Rita Fairclough."

I looked up to find a very tall young man, kitted out in jeans and denim jacket, looking admiringly down at me over a packet of fish and chips. He offered me a chip which I declined and, after disillusioning him as politely as I could, I stifled a smile as I excused myself and went off to find a taxi.

I enjoyed the ride across London, seeing the sights and chatting to the driver. I found that if you are going to a television studio they always ask you which programme you are on and the driver was interested in UFOs. I was not aware until that day that taxi drivers do give receipts for the fare and as this one included the tip as well, I was later to be grateful to him as no expenses were paid unless receipts were forthcoming.

After announcing my arrival at the reception desk, a group of us were guided along passages, through large storage rooms and up stairs to the hospitality room where there were plates of sandwiches, tea, coffee, orange juice and milk to refresh weary travellers.

Apart from a young girl, I was the only lady there at that time and as she needed the loo I volunteered to take her, and quite an adventure it was with stairs and corridors to contend with. This probably would not have been so memorable had it not been that when we returned the men present had eaten all the sandwiches and more had to be brought along.

Many more people arrived for the programme, fifty-four in all. It was rather crowded in that small room but soon it was as if I had known everyone for a long time. When ufologists and UFO witnesses get together it can be guaranteed that experiences will soon be exchanged. At that time I was not aware who most of them were, but I had met Jenny and she introduced me to some of them. Everyone seemed to know my name and what had happened to me.

During this time those of us who had been scripted to take an active part in the programme were called into another room and told the point at which we would be brought into the discussion. I was scheduled to be introduced about fifteen minutes into it and following a lady named Linda. I returned to the room to find that Robert Kilroy-Silk had joined the group and soon afterwards we made our way upwards in lifts, which carried a maximum of twenty people, to the recording studio. My first impression of that was that the many overhanging lights were very appropriate to a discussion on UFOs.

The seating arrangement had been planned and we were ushered to our seats. Details of fire prevention rules were given and the programme details were explained. We were told when to clap and a trailer was made to advertise the next morning's programme. Then we were ready to start having been told that if we wanted to contribute to the programme we were to put up our hands and Robert would come along with his microphone.

Recording went along smoothly with me waiting patiently to be brought into the discussion fifteen minutes later. I watched Linda knowing that I would be next. But no, she was not spoken to and when the section on close encounters was introduced my heart skipped a beat. I thought, 'Here I go', but no, it was not to be. A Yorkshire policeman, Alan Godfrey, told his story and I was forgotten. At one point where I thought I could contribute I put up my hand but Robert's attention was elsewhere and in no time at all the forty minutes were up. We filed out of the studio, into the lifts then back to the hospitality room for wine and nibbles and to collect our expenses on the production of receipts. Afterwards a fleet of cars took us to our respective destinations and at 6.15 p.m. I arrived in Burnt Oak where I was to stay the night with my son, Douglas, his wife Rose and the grandchildren, Terri-Jayne and Stuart.

Many friends and villagers had watched the programme expecting to see me telling my story. "Never mind," they very kindly said, "we did see you wave to us."

For a time it seemed like a wasted journey but really it was to prepare me well for future television appearances, also I had now met Jenny Randles who was to become a very good friend. I had realised that the interest in UFOs really was world-wide and I had met many people who in later years were, in one way or another, to become increasingly involved in my life. Another pathway had been opened to me.

Chapter Eight

PROMISED A RETURN VISIT?

Never in my wildest dreams could I have imagined on 22nd November 1978 that nine years later my name would have been known to so many people. I found that Jenny had already described my sighting in one of her previous books, *UFO Reality*. Our middle son, David, had used my account of it with a discussion group in London and it became one of the Reading Prediction Exercises used by students at Nene College in Northampton. My brother had a number of friends equally interested and there were all those who knew me and were following my developments with enthusiasm. Of course, giving BUFORA permission to use my name on the investigation forms was mostly the reason for this and local publicity through newspapers and radio helped too.

Nor on the 30th April 1984, the day on which I officially retired through ill-health, could I have imagined that in January 1988 I would be anything but a helpless arthritic. During the year after retiring, I had got steadily worse and eventually came to the point where I had to be helped in and out of a car.

It was then I decided that as conventional medicine could only offer painkillers, I would become unconventional. My mother's policy health-wise had always been to cure ourselves if at all possible. So I decided to try it. I read many books on the subject and learned as much as I could. Then I had my allergies to eight different foods sorted out with acupuncture and put myself on an anti-arthritic diet which I was convinced would work. To supplement this I joined a slimming group and it was there that I met Joan Pearson who was to become a firm friend, though neither of us realised at that time that about six years previously, after she had read about it in the *Chronicle & Echo* newspaper, it was she who had rung me to talk about my sighting.

I lost two stones in weight. Dancing and walking became less painful and my confidence gradually returned, so that by the time Jenny came into my life I was much fitter and ready to take on a completely new challenge – to understand the reasons for that encounter with a UFO nine years before, to find out if I was in some way selected and if so, for what reason?

This, I was to find, would entail a lot more publicity, some kind and some quite shocking, but I also found that no matter how it came I always seemed to have the strength and dignity to cope with it.

I waited eagerly for Jenny's book to be published and during this time I was told to expect a call from *She* magazine which was to publish an article about the book and would want a photograph to accompany it. My case was to be one of those described in the article.

Whilst I was waiting for that call Jenny asked me to join her on the 5th May 1988 as she was to do a programme for Radio Wales. I was happy that here was another opportunity to increase my knowledge about UFOs. I still had read no books on the subject. Information was coming incidentally. I would have liked an explanation of the reasons for my encounter but saw no need then to make a specific effort to find one. One day, I felt sure, it would happen.

At BBC Radio Northampton a link-up had been arranged with Jenny in a studio at Radio Manchester. We were both having a 'down the line' interview with Frank Hennesy for the 'Street Life' programme on Radio Wales.

The programme was introduced with a series of questions setting the scene for me to describe my close encounter. "Do you believe in the theory of life on other planets? Have you ever looked up at a starry sky and wondered whether somebody up there is looking back at you across the great universe and wondering exactly the same thing?" I thought it was a very appropriate question. I had often looked up and wondered myself, but somehow never expected anyone up there to be thinking I might be doing the same thing down here.

I learned that the first documented sighting of a UFO was made in 1947, over forty years ago. Then I was introduced as someone who had not only seen a UFO but who had actually experienced contact with alien beings.

That was going to take a bit of getting used to – 'contact with alien beings'. I had got over the original embarrassment when it happened, but in Jenny's book she had said that my 'beings' could be taken for 'people'. I now expected more public ridicule, but I had coped before and I felt I could do so again. I decided to cross that bridge if and when I came to it.

After relating my account, the presenter said that he had found it very exciting as he had never spoken to anyone who had had an encounter before. "It's obviously a terrifying thing and the memories of it will remain with you for the rest of your life," he said.

In explaining why my case was important, Jenny said that I was very brave because I was prepared to talk about it, that 'this was a tremendous thing to do as it was an experience which has a very deep trauma on the witness and it is extremely difficult for them to talk for fear of the ridicule it will create.' She also said that the sighting later in the evening by the four ladies at Preston Capes gave a degree of corroboration way beyond coincidence and certainly suggested that something lay behind both experiences.

The presenter was interested in my unaccountable fifteen minutes and it was explained that this was the way in which abductions are discovered, also that abductions were actually called 'Close Encounters of the Fourth Kind'. Conventional sightings reported in Britain each year may number 600 or more but only one or two abductees are heard about. They are extremely rare and when they are reported the witnesses are studied by psychologists, psychiatrists and sociologists as I had been. In the majority of cases they are found to be sincere.

Sometimes telepathic messages are communicated to the witnesses by the aliens. Usually they are of an ecological nature and express concern for the state of the planet. How much easier it would be to understand if someone could take a good photograph of a UFO or its occupants, or perhaps bring back a souvenir after an abduction.

* * *

After the publication of Jenny's book there were distribution problems and the photograph was never taken, so it happened that I saw and read the article before the book.

'I was kidnapped by an aliens from outer space' read the heading on the cover of the June 1988 issue of *She* magazine and I longed to read about it. Inside under the heading of 'Features' it said, "I was abducted by an alien and lived to tell the tale, say some (very sane) people." On page seventy-two we were 'very down-to-earth' people and I learned that scientists were beginning to take us seriously, which, after the experience of my actual sighting and the public reaction following it, was very welcome news.

I read the article and to say that my initial reaction was one of shock was an understatement. Alien rape was a thing I had never heard of and to learn that it was thought that I had missed that experience because I was past child-bearing age at the time seemed too incredible to be true. I had heard something about genetic experimentation and 'wise baby dreams' on the Radio Wales programme, but as I was sure that nothing like that had happened to me, I had not taken much notice of it.

The article also stated that when I was put under hypnosis I recalled alien shapes (which I did) beside the UFO (which I didn't) and that I had said that I had been 'selected, scanned, promised a return visit, then ultimately rejected'.

One expects articles on this subject to be sensational but, over the years my story has never varied. Therefore I was amazed to read that I had been 'promised a return visit'. My initial reaction to this article, which was accompanied by a picture of an alien bending over a naked woman, was one of anger. But, on reflection, I wondered if I should have taken it so seriously. After all, how could anyone who had not experienced what I had, know exactly how I felt? So, after John had read it, we decided that we would not treat it too seriously and eventually I joked to others who had read it about 'missing a fate worse than death because of old age!'

It is thought in UFO circles that if you are over thirty-five you are safe from abduction by aliens in a UFO. I was forty-nine at the time and this, it was assumed, was the reason I had been rejected.

Of course I now know that this type of abduction does take place and a very traumatic experience it must be, but on that day I was very naive on the subject of UFOs and had read the article expecting that all time lapses involved something similar to what had probably happened to me. Yet, in that article it appeared that it was so, because the selection of samples used was on the theme of genetic experimentation. But, because I had not felt any fear on the day of the encounter I had assumed that 'they' were friendly and meant me no harm. Even though under hypnosis I was terrified, as the years went by I put that down to the fact that those 'beings' were such an unusual shape and that so many things were alien to my understanding. All this had to be put into some kind of perspective in order to find an explanation for what could have happened to me during the time lapse.

Eventually I received a copy of Jenny's book and eagerly read it, hoping to find details of another sighting similar to mine. This was my main objective. Nearly ten years had elapsed and I now felt that I needed someone to talk to who had experienced a similar encounter and who could really understand how I felt.

I expected someone else to have seen red and green lights, but no; a dumb-bell shaped object – no; darkness – no; flashing circles of brilliant white light – no. The only things I had in common with many other abductees, as we were now being called, were the interference with the electronics of the car, the distance the car travelled without the driver being in control and a time loss.

My encounter had been described locally as the most spectacular sighting in Northamptonshire. I now began to believe that this could be so, but it is hard to come to terms with the fact that it could be so special and yet still know so little about the reasons for it.

I could not understand why it had been written that I had been 'promised a return visit'. It bothered me a lot. To the best of my knowledge I had never said that. Had it come out under hypnosis? It was true that I had never heard the tapes of that session, nor had I been given a transcript afterwards.

But then, I was expecting another session and assumed that I would know all about it then, so perhaps I had been told. It was now nine years since I had been hypnotised. I had still read no books on the subject and really, until Jenny's book was published, I was happily believing that it was all over. Just a 'one-off' never to be repeated.

But now I began to wonder, was all this in order to open my mind and bring a new awareness to me of what was planned for the future?

Chapter Nine

REMINDERS?

Slowly and really unconsciously I was increasing my knowledge about UFOs, but not intentionally in the expectation that I would need the information, I could not see any reason to need it, but I still wanted to understand what had happened to me. That part I did need to know to put the mystery to rest.

My friend, Joan Pearson, was optimistic. "Perhaps you were promised a return visit," she said one day, "maybe that is what all this is about? Perhaps they want you to realise that they are still around and that they've not forgotten you."

Well, strange things do happen which we can't explain. I discussed it with members at the Northampton UFO Group meetings. I had heard that some abductees had been promised return visits but usually had been given a time, sometimes ten years on. Some had been given other information that they would not remember until a certain time had passed. Had these things perhaps happened to me?

There was no reason why something like that could not have happened as I sat looking at those brilliant white circles of light in the darkness. Perhaps they had been a decoy to take my mind off what really occurred. But why would they want to see me again? Had I not felt that I had been rejected? Hadn't the supposition been that I was too old for their experiments?

I think that deep down Joan hoped it might be true that contact had not been lost, but my feelings were not so enthusiastic. However, during 1988 several things occurred which gave us food for thought.

In February of that year another appearance on television had been organised. This time it was to be on Central Television and I had to travel to Nottingham for a live programme called 'The Time – The Place'. As with Kilroy, I had several calls on the previous afternoon to ensure that the researchers had every point in my story accurate and I had been assured that I would make a contribution as my experience would definitely be included.

Arriving at the British Rail station in Nottingham, I found that the taxi rank had been moved as Prince Charles was also paying a visit to the city on that day. I was being guided to its new position by a policeman when a man behind me, who I recognised from the Kilroy programme, asked if I was going to Central TV. He followed and we shared the same taxi. It was a journey which I have never forgotten. I was sitting by the driver and he sat behind us.

"Have you had a sighting?" he suddenly asked as we travelled.

"Yes," I replied.

"Were you examined?"

"I don't know."

"Have you any scars?"

"Scars? Where?"

"Behind your knees."

By this time I was feeling very embarrassed and the driver must have wondered what on earth we were talking about.

"That's a place I don't look at very often," I answered and hastily changed the subject to include the driver in the conversation.

Unfortunately the morning proved to be almost a copy of the Kilroy programme. Once again I had been prepared but my story was not used. As I had had to travel about thirty miles to Kettering Station in the early hours of the morning in order to catch a train which would enable me to arrive at the studio just after nine o'clock, it was a very tired and disappointed abductee who returned just after lunch.

That day I had been impressed with the British Rail service. It was a different line from the one I usually used from Northampton. The coaches were all so clean, the seats were so comfortable and both journeys had been very smooth. Having got up early that morning, the excitement of taking part in a live television broadcast and the disappointment of not saying a word again had all contributed to an overwhelming desire to sleep. But, not being familiar with the route, I decided it would be better to stay awake and be sure that I got off the train at the right station.

Perhaps I had relaxed too much, because all of a sudden I was jolted into the realisation that I had a possible answer to one of the many

74

questions I had been left with after my hypnosis.

Why did the circle of brilliant white light come towards me and what was it doing?

I had asked myself this question many times. Now I wondered, was I being X-rayed? But for what reason? Perhaps that was all that did happen, but I had a strange feeling that I was one step further forward in my search for the answers I needed and I found myself thinking through the experience of the sighting in minute detail.

On the way home from the station John and I called in to see Joan and her husband Frank to tell them about the programme. They, like many other villagers, friends and relatives had watched it hoping to hear Church Stowe mentioned and had been disappointed again.

* * *

In August 1988 our youngest son, Douglas, and his family moved from their home in London and came to live in Weedon, just two miles away from Church Stowe and in the village where I had first seen my UFO.

Two months later, Terri-Jayne our grand-daughter and her friend were playing together. It was just before 6.00 p.m. and time for the friend to go home. Terri went with her, pushing her bicycle up the hill.

As they reached her friend's house they saw something unusual in the sky, a very bright white light which they later described as 'eye-shaped'. Her friend was not interested and went into her house whilst Terri watched. The light zig-zagged into the distance and disappeared. Terri rode her bicycle home.

There, as she was about to put it into the garage, she looked up to see a more colourful 'thing' above her next-door-neighbour's house. This was also white and eye-shaped but had lights coloured red, blue, green and yellow around the centre of it. On the top there was a light which flashed alternately red and blue and underneath was a black area. Terri described it as being as big as a van and about half a house higher than the neighbour's house.

It was completely stationary and Terri shouted for her mother to come and see it but before she arrived the black area at the bottom had changed to white and all the coloured lights had gone out. It became a brilliant white eye-shaped object and "zoomed off to the right".

Terri did not understand what she had seen. She was very frightened and that frightened her mother. Even so, it was several days before they told me about it.

Having had an even closer encounter myself, I was able to talk her through her experience and compare it to mine. She had known previously that I had seen a UFO but she did not know all the details. Her parents had a copy of Jenny's book, *Abduction,* but Terri had never read it. To take away some of the terror I said that we were both special and it brought us even closer together as this was something new which we had in common.

As the Daventry area's representative for the Northamptonshire UFO Research Centre and therefore responsible for reporting sightings in the area, I informed the Secretary, Ernest Still, about Terri's sightings and learned from him that on that day similar objects had been seen in other areas of the country.

Terri's sightings had been at Weedon at 6.00 p.m. Five minutes later there were three separate sightings of a group of six objects over Northampton and at 6.25 p.m. there were another three reports of a group of three objects over Corby, these seen by Ernest himself. A few days after this he told me that later that same evening they were observed over Leicestershire as well.

To know that she was not the only one to see them was a great comfort to Terri. Ernest sent the UFO Sighting Account Forms to fill in and with her parents present I helped her to complete them. They were the same as those I had received so the task was not too daunting.

Ernest was eager to know if anyone else in Weedon had seen anything on that evening and Terri bravely told the *Daventry Weekly Express* reporters about it. I warned her that some of the children at school would probably make fun of her but she assured me she could cope with it.

The photograph in the newspaper showed her pointing to the sky and this was the pose that some of the children met her with as she arrived at school the following Monday morning. Anyone who was rude, she said, was jealous because they had not seen the objects. Her teacher encouraged her to tell the class about it and she wrote the story and drew pictures too. She had a very understanding teacher. Then later, more interest was raised when she went with me to appear with Jenny on the 'Ghost Train' programme for Border Television.

The date of this sighting was 24th October 1988 and Terri was ten and a half years old. It was about three weeks before the tenth anniversary of my sighting and it was about 200 yards as the crow flies from where I had driven under that dumb-bell-shaped object.

* * *

Following my weekly shampoo and blow-dry, I often visit Joan, who I now consider to be a very special friend. During the visit, following my trip to Central TV's 'The Time – The Place' programme, I had told her about the conversation I'd had in the taxi on the way to the studio.

On this occasion, following Terri's sighting, Joan was excited. "It's strange," she said, "I've just been reading about someone who saw a UFO and found afterwards she had a scar on her leg." She found the newspaper and read the description. It was circular, just behind and below the knee and it had a dip in the centre.

It was no good. I had to own up. I had a scar in the same place. It was the same shape and it fitted the description in every detail, also it was after my sighting that I had noticed it. It was definitely not there before my encounter but this was not to say that the occupants of the UFO, if there were some, were responsible for it. I had always thought that it had been caused by an earwig which had crawled up into the leg of my jeans whilst gardening. I had not told many people about it, but not one of those who had seen it would believe that an earwig could cause a mark that size.

At the time Joan was not aware that I had this scar so here was a good opportunity to get another opinion. On inspection we could only agree that the one described in the newspaper and mine were identical. To this day I still give the earwig the credit for it, but Joan had another theory. She was still intrigued, as was I about 'being promised a return visit' and she had reasoned out a possible explanation which could cover the happenings of 1988.

"Perhaps you were promised a return visit, or given information that you would only remember at a later date, and the things that have been happening this year are to prepare you for this," she volunteered and continued, "to remind you that they are still around and are still interested in you?" What a thought-provoking comment that turned out to be.

- Was my memory of what occurred on 22nd November 1978 fading and needed a jolt or two to rekindle it?
- Had Jenny's book been a vehicle that was used to awaken my interest

and to make me think deeply about the reasons for my abduction?
- Was that earwig meant to draw my attention to a scar on my leg?
- Then there was Terri's sighting.

If I needed persuading that they were still around, to appear for my grand-daughter in almost the same spot as they had waited for me, almost ten years to the day later, how could I but notice that they were still around and wonder if there was a purpose behind it all?

I had always assumed that a return visit, if one were intended, would be in exactly the same form as the original one, that one day when I turned onto the A5 at Weedon another dumb-bell-shaped object would be there above the road and that I would have a similar experience.

This, of course, is based on an assumption put forward by a human mind, but I am not dealing with human beings, am I? I am dealing with supposed extraterrestrial beings whose ways of behaviour and reasoning would not necessarily match ours, so who is to say that I have not already had my return visit and that it was in such a form that my human mind interpreted it as a reminder? I mean of course when Terri was visited in the same village.

But then, the craft was a different shape. So what? On earth we change cars, some of us many times within a ten-year period and in space travel the vehicle would also be more up to date ten years later. It had a dark area underneath, perhaps an opening of some kind. I saw nothing as elaborate as that on my UFO. But it's a theory worth considering and could be part of the reasons for the renewal of my interest in the subject around that time.

Chapter Ten

NUFORC

When I had my close encounter in 1978, I had great difficulty in finding an official body to whom I could report it – but not so when Terri needed help. Immediate contact was made with the Northampton UFO Research Centre (NUFORC).

The centre was formed on the 4th day of July 1987 by Ernest Still from Corby and Susan Pollock from Northampton. Ernest was Northamptonshire's representative for BUFORA and became the first chairman of NUFORC. Susan was NUFORC's first secretary. Clive Potter from Leicester, who was BUFORA's regional investigations co-ordinator, also assisted in the formation of the group whose aim was to form a network of investigators in Northamptonshire and Leicestershire which would co-operate with other groups and organisations in the Midlands area.

I first heard about this organisation in another surprise phone call which I received from Reg Pinckheard. It was he who had come into the Teachers' Centre to talk about my sighting just after it had happened and whom I met occasionally over the years when shopping in Daventry. He asked if I knew that a UFO group had been set up in Northampton and whether I minded him giving my address and telephone number to the secretary as he thought I would be interested.

To be honest I was not very enthusiastic. After all, it was a research centre and what did I know about research into UFOs? But I said I didn't mind and waited to find out where, if anywhere, I would fit into the organisation.

Following this, I received a phone call from Ernest. He knew about my sighting and asked if I would attend their next meeting and talk to their members about it. The meeting was to be on Saturday 14th

November 1987 from 1.30 to 4.00 p.m. and by 4.00 p.m. it would be getting dark. I was beginning by that time to get back a little confidence in driving but still did not like travelling alone.

I knew that John would not be coming with me, he would be elsewhere on that day and at that time I knew of no-one else who would be interested enough. I had not driven in the dark for a few years and did not know the area where the meeting was to be held. A battle went on inside me. I felt I should go, but would I find the place? More important, would I get back safely as it would be a Saturday and there would be the football traffic to contend with? Looking back – how negative all this was. I heard Ernest saying he would send me a map of the Weston Favell area of Northampton – and I heard myself saying that I would go.

Billingbrooke Road was easy enough to find once I had negotiated the ring road, a new experience for me driving on my own again, and I arrived in good time for the meeting. This was to be another first, being one of a group of like-minded people genuinely interested in UFOs and wanting, like me, to understand more about the phenomenon. Perhaps among these people, who obviously had delved into the subject more deeply than I had and who had been interested in it a great deal longer than I had, there would be answers to some of my questions? I couldn't have been made more welcome. I was put at ease immediately.

The tables had been set out as were those at Teachers' Centre meetings and I was given a place of honour at the top. One young man, who introduced himself as Clive Potter, asked if I minded him taping what I said. Knowing Clive well now as the regional investigator for the group, that tape recorder must have travelled many, many miles with him and recorded countless interviews.

I gave an account of my sighting, the tightening sensations around my head, the hypnosis and Jenny's phone call. Then, as questions flowed and suggestions were made I found that I really was enjoying the company – a group of people all talking about UFOs and what is more, believing in them. This really was new to me and I was glad I had made the effort to go.

I was in two minds whether to tell them about Jenny's experiment, but decided to do so and this prompted more suggestions – the one standing out most being from another young man named David Rogers. He asked if I were at all psychic as head sensations such as I had described were often experienced by those who were. Then he asked whether it had occurred to me that the tightening sensation around my head at lunch time on the day of my close encounter could have been the 'occupants' of the UFO tuning into my subconscious and telling me that they were going to have a closer look at me on the way home, and that I would not be afraid.

For some reason which I can't explain this has always made sense. Why else would I be completely fascinated by something which, if I had heard about it before, would have been too scarey for words?

Ernest insisted on giving me £5 towards my travelling expenses which I found most embarrassing, so as it was a new group and subscriptions were due at that meeting, I decided to give it back to him and become a member – and without realising it at the time, it was the beginning of a quest to find out more about UFOs and more important to find someone else who had had a similar experience to mine and with whom I could compare notes.

After all the hesitation and lack of confidence in my ability to get there alone, it was a very enjoyable and rewarding meeting and of course I drove home full of exciting thoughts and with no trouble at all. My confidence in driving alone was beginning to return.

Becoming a member of NUFORC has turned out to be one of the best things I could have done in order to find answers to my questions. It has led to meeting many other people, some of whom have had sightings and some who wish they had, also members of other societies who are equally interested in trying to understand what is happening and why.

The aims of the Northampton UFO Research Centre are to encourage investigation and research into UFO phenomena; to collect evidence and data relating to it; to co-ordinate UFO research in Northampton and the Midlands and to co-operate with persons and organisations engaged upon similar research in all parts of Britain and the rest of the world. There are the usual officers – Chairman, Vice-chairman, Secretary and Treasurer and we have a Newsletter Editor, a Director of Research, an Investigations Co-ordinator with an Investigation Team and Area Representatives in each part of the county. I represent the Daventry area and pass on to the Secretary details of any sightings I hear about, whether within my area or outside. Friends and relatives send cuttings from newspapers and these are all forwarded to be used in the research.

Since joining, Joan, who became a member soon afterwards, and I look forward to the two-monthly meetings now held in the centre of Northampton not far from the bus station. Terri has also attended some of them and they were a great help in getting her to talk about her sighting more freely. She also enjoyed helping to prepare and serve the refreshments when we stopped for a break.

I have learned a great deal there about BUFORA and decided at the end of 1988 to become a member. The British UFO Research Association's aims are to investigate all reports of UFO sightings and to carry out scientific research into every aspect on the subject. It was founded in 1964 and incorporated the London UFO Research Organisation, which was the pioneer of UFO research in Great Britain from 1959.

Of special interest to me is the fact that the Association is looking into all cases of reported sightings during November 1978. This will include my close encounter and I look forward to reading the published report.

NUFORC's present Chairman, Steve Gamble, is also the Director of Research for BUFORA. He and Ernest, who became the NUFORC Secretary and Treasurer have, as part of a team completed an analysis of the Northamptonshire UFO reports from 1950 to 1988. This was recorded in the Journal of Transient Aerial Phenomena, published by BUFORA in March 1989.

Some of the members of NUFORC are accredited BUFORA investigators also, but we are one and all just ordinary members of the public, who not only have an interest in UFOs but also in a vast range of subjects not connected with them. This makes discussions more objective and hopefully will enable us to come to some kind of understanding of the phenomenon – if there is one to be found.

Chapter Eleven

EUPHORIA

In the six months from February to July 1989 my life changed completely and I can only describe myself as having been in a state of euphoria. Nothing at all worried me, no matter what it was. I reacted with the same calmness however urgent an occasion seemed to be to other people. It was a wonderful feeling and the serenity I felt was matched only by that experienced for a few weeks after December 1968 when John was promoted to Town Sergeant and we had to move from the village of Loddington to live in Daventry.

For seventeen years I had been a village policeman's wife and in those days the village office, which was attached to the house, was in use for twenty-four hours a day every day of the week and to members of the public who needed a policeman urgently, when John was out on duty, I was expected to have all the answers and be able to deal with their problems. Also it was expected that incoming messages from other police stations were competently accepted and passed on to be dealt with when contact could be made with John. I was very tired at that time and would have liked to have taken a term away from teaching. I had been working full-time for thirteen years since our third son Douglas was born and, with only occasional help in the house from a delightful lady from Rothwell, I felt that a move to another part of the county would have been an ideal opportunity to take a term's rest before applying for a new teaching post. But that was not to be.

Up to that point it had been relatively easy to get a teaching transfer to whichever area we moved to, but at that particular time the first three-year trained students would soon be joining the profession and it would not have been wise to take time off during the spring term, when there would be a flood of newly-qualified teachers completing their courses in the summer. Reasoning then in the educational world was that these new teachers would be better trained than we older ones had been with only two years of training and would also be cheaper to employ than those of us higher up the salary scale. So it seemed wiser for me to carry on and I hoped that a change would really be 'as good as a rest'.

To ensure that I could do this I had visited my doctor and had been prescribed what every stressed person of the 1960s was prescribed – tranquillisers. Mine were amphetamines and very relaxing they were too. I am often reminded about the time we had all arrived home from our various schools, the boys had done their paper rounds and we sat discussing our respective days. Suddenly the subject changed.

"I don't know what those tablets are that you are on, Mum," said my fifteen-year-old, "but they're jolly good whatever they are."

"Why?" I asked nonchalantly.

"Because I've been sitting here with my feet up on this chair for about half an hour," he answered triumphantly, "and you haven't said a word!"

I could not have cared less. I was at peace with the world and with everyone in it. Happily for me though my new doctor said that amphetamines were addictive. I was soon weaned away from them and quickly gained control of my own life once more. Now, this was exactly how I felt again, so tranquil and so happy. Someone, somewhere had obviously decided that I should be at ease with my surroundings, at peace with everyone I came into contact with and well prepared for any task ahead of me. This was to be a period of enlightenment where UFOs were concerned, a time when I was to find myself involved in radio and television interviews and attending an International Congress.

* * *

The 10th of February 1989 saw me travelling along the M1 with John Spencer, the present Chairman of BUFORA. He had asked me to accompany him on a programme to be broadcast by his local radio station at their Luton studios.

"The lady's flipped her lid. She's completely off her trolley – out of her tree!"

These were the thoughts which Gerald Maine felt the Radio Bedfordshire listeners might have following the description of my encounter which I had given at the start of the programme. He had listened carefully and patiently to what he called a "remarkable story", then he offered suggestions which both he and I hoped would explain what had happened.

It was difficult to understand why no-one else had reported seeing my dumb-bell-shaped UFO stationary above one of the busiest roads in the country. Church Stowe is in an area where military and civilian aircraft continually cross the skies and international flights pass over Daventry, seven miles away. We are surrounded by air bases of various kinds and take very little notice of the number of aircraft which fly daily above the village. Even so, I was sure that none of those would offer a logical explanation for what I had seen.

He wondered if it had lead me to think that it could have been an hallucination on my part, or the result of something I had eaten, or drunk, even some illness I might have had – all suggestions which had been made to me many times before. No, there was no way I had been able to explain it as one of these, but I did hope that John had a logical answer. At that moment my hopes were really high.

John is a researcher and has written several books on the subject of UFOs. He has had no encounters himself but his work often takes him abroad and just before the programme he had visited Brussels and Sweden to talk to ufologists and witnesses there. So, he had a lot of information on which to draw. But he did not have an answer, only an encouraging statistic. He explained that if I had "flipped my lid" or was "off my trolley" then that description would fit possibly 10,000 people in this country and maybe 100,000 in America, as it is thought that number of people have similar stories to tell.

I was also happy to hear that investigations had been going on for forty years into stories similar to mine and that investigators had often received accounts of missing time periods, strange lights and close encounters with strange, unidentifiable objects. After ten years I had still met no-one who had experienced a similar encounter and it was very gratifying to know that I was not alone.

I described people's reactions on hearing my story. Originally they had been many and varied, but since Jenny's book had been published the ridicule had subsided quite a lot. People who had known me for years could see that I had not changed. In fact I had worked very hard to cover up my true feelings. But as I was speaking to a fellow dancer at a class during the week before this interview, another man had hovered. He heard us talking about UFOs.

"Surely you don't believe that rubbish?" he suddenly asked, looking me straight in the eyes. Then he roared with laughter.

I waited for it to subside, then I looked him in the eyes and calmly said, "if it had happened to you, *you* would." That obviously gave him something to think about and since that night I am able to discuss the subject rationally with him whenever he chooses to mention it.

John was asked some very searching questions that day and gave equally thorough and detailed answers. I listened intently and found that I could relate to many points which were raised. For example, I could only agree that it did not appear to be logical that if we were being visited by entities from another planet, galaxy or dimension, who really did not want to make contact with us, that they mostly appeared to single people, often at night and very secretly. It would have been much more sensible to manifest themselves to millions at the same time by appearing during a popular television show.

Types of cases were discussed and the feelings of those who are involved with them. John felt that I did not seem to have suffered from my encounter, that it had fascinated me and had possibly enriched me in many ways. However, many abductees relate experiences similar to rape, are terrified afterwards and find they have great difficulty in continuing to live normal lives. The more I hear, the luckier I feel. I am sure I met with friendly 'beings'.

Most people have heard of the film *Close Encounters of the Third Kind* but we were talking about a Fourth Kind – Gerald Maine was not the only one who was confused. I was equally pleased to hear the definitions given to the different categories of UFO sightings.

There are two basic types – distant encounters and close encounters.

Distant encounters are of objects seen in the sky and of night lights, obviously the only way they can be noticed in darkness.

Close encounters have four categories:

- First Kind – when an object can be seen in the sky and it is close enough for the witness to realise that it is not an identifiable aircraft;
- Second Kind – where physical traces are left by some kind of object, perhaps because it has landed;
- Third Kind – where there is a one-to-one meeting with the occupants of the object;
- Fourth Kind – which are really abductions, when the witness experiences a loss of time and some report that they have been taken on board for a variety of reasons.

I learned that local authorities are very co-operative when the investigators are trying to find answers to the strange encounters which members of the public report. Co-operation from local airports is given where an answer is required relating to lights in the sky. The 'Stealth' aircraft have been seen and believed to be UFOs. They have been the cause of many reported sightings.

It is thought in many circles too that the government has been covering up UFO reports for many years. I have no idea what they did with the one I sent. I always assumed it would be filed somewhere, but obviously they would need to determine whether there would be any threat to national security before doing so. In fact some witnesses who now report sightings to the Ministry of Defence are referred to BUFORA, whose investigators look into them very thoroughly.

The first stage of investigation is the type which I have described in Chapter three when those of us with strange experiences to describe hope to be supplied with answers at the end of it. In many cases, perhaps 90 to 95% of them, answers can be found, but in those like mine there seems to be no explanation.

John Spencer works on the next level of this investigative process. He collates large numbers of reports and examines them critically, hoping to find a common thread which will lead to a greater understanding of the many questions still unanswered, some of them being: "What are these UFOs?" and "From where do they come?" Perhaps also there may be a common factor among the witnesses? Many, many questions needing answers and many, many people like me hoping they will soon be found.

"Do you think you will crack what actually happened that night?" I was asked at the end of the programme.

"I think so," I answered and felt very confident as I qualified it by adding that I thought that what had happened to me was just one tiny piece in a very large jigsaw puzzle.

I had always felt that an answer to all this was out there somewhere and that I would eventually find why I had been chosen to be part of this great mystery. I had talked about a jigsaw puzzle and indeed it did seem to be so. I was to find later that I was not the only person to be using that definition, which had come into my mind just before the programme.

Again I was told that it had taken "a lot of guts" to actually admit something like that, but I still felt that by talking about it to other people on radio, television, or wherever the opportunity presented itself, someone would be able to fit my small piece of the jigsaw into its place and eventually we would see the reasons for all these encounters.

Chapter Twelve

A TELEVISION APPEAL

By Easter 1989 *Abduction* had been printed in paperback, and I was again accompanying Jenny on the promotion trail. This time, however, it was quite different, just the two of us and I was more involved in the programmes.

It was a time when, looking back, it seemed as if there was a reason for my inclusion. I only expected each time to have to relate my story, but before each programme questions came into my mind which seemed important enough to be asked of a wider audience. On each occasion I found I was given the opportunity and some of the results were to have far-reaching effects into the future.

During the afternoon of 28th March 1989 I had been collected by a taxi to be driven to Liverpool where I was to take part in a programme for Granada TV.

"You must be a very important lady," the taxi driver had said, "they don't usually send taxis this far." He was interested in UFOs and as I sat in his front passenger seat and we travelled along the motorways, the conversation flowed and made the long journey most enjoyable.

Jenny would be there too to talk about her book and the viewers had been asked to phone in questions about UFOs. As the programme was to be an early one, I was to stay overnight in a hotel so that I could be at the studio for 9.30 the following morning. This was indeed luxury.

At 9.15 the following morning I was collected by taxi and taken to the Wharf Studio of Granada Television. This was alongside the Albert Docks and quite literally a window on the world, where passers-by could look in on the activities of the studio as they walked to the shops built along the dockside.

The programme was called 'This Morning'. It was presented by the husband and wife team of Judy Finnegan and Richard Madely and went out on all ITV channels. The section in which we were involved was a phone-in and earlier, and on the previous day, viewers had been asked to telephone with questions and comments about UFOs. Jenny and I had seen those which had already arrived, between twenty and thirty of them, and Jenny selected about six which covered a range of interests. We particularly wanted to include one from a child and there were two amongst them. To ensure they were not hoaxes, the telephonist said she would ring the numbers given and speak to the parents. Then, if they supported the original calls the questions could be included in the programme.

A final selection of four questions was made by the programme researcher from the short-list prepared earlier. We did not know which questions they were as the programme started, but sadly there was not one from a child so perhaps no parents were at home to verify their child's supposed sighting.

Jenny had been introduced as one of Britain's leading experts on UFOs and I was introduced as having claimed to have met an alien, all designed no doubt to hold an audience captive.

The whole programme had been planned in minute detail as regards time and there was not enough allowed for me to describe the whole experience, so Richard condensed most of it and put the emphasis on to the aliens. I was then asked if I was absolutely certain that my experience was something to do with aliens from another planet. Wow! How was I to answer that one?

Here for the first time I was in contact with someone who obviously believed that I had met aliens, something which I have never claimed to have done. This emphasis came as quite a shock. It is true that I had used the word 'alien' in the past, but only in the context that the ghost-like shapes which I had seen under hypnosis 'were alien to my understanding' at the time – and for that matter, still are. So I explained that the word 'alien' is interpreted in a different way by each of us and described briefly what I had seen and that the whole experience was still unexplained and I could not find an answer myself. For that reason I had been grateful that I had been put in touch with BUFORA. But now ten years later, and having read Jenny's book from cover to cover in the hope that I might find someone else who had had a similar experience (and not doing so) I felt an urgency to talk to someone who had, so that we could compare notes.

Then, what a surprise, Judy appealed to the viewers. "If anyone has had a similar experience to Elsie's," she said, "I am sure she would love to hear from you. Let us know about it and we will put you in touch with her."

And that is exactly what happened. About four weeks later I received a letter from Jenny enclosing one from a viewer. He told me that he had seen the programme and that something very similar to my experience had happened to him in 1979. Since the involvement with *Abduction*, I had felt the need to understand what had happened much more strongly and now here was someone else who had been in that very situation. He did not give details of his sighting but seemed to understand the difficulties that I was meeting in finding the answers. He said he knew that he could be of help in assisting me to find the truth, if I so wished, but he left it to my discretion as to whether or not I contacted him.

If I have an important decision to make I always sleep on it first. Things always seem to be more logical and more easily accomplished at the beginning of a new day, so I contained my excitement and decided to do just that.

The letter was the answer to a prayer. Obviously here was someone who knew a great deal more about the reasons for a UFO abduction than I did. Perhaps now I would find the answers to those questions which had been haunting me for the last ten years. Having slept on it, there was no doubt in my mind that I should take advantage of the offer in the hope that it would clarify the situation at last.

How simple it all seemed to be that morning. In my mind I composed a reply to the letter whilst doing my household chores and was already getting excited about receiving a reply. This, however, was to happen sooner than expected. Graham Allen phoned me before the letter had been completed and I learned that his abduction experience really was in many ways similar to mine.

He had been driving a Renault (as was I) on a lovely sunny day when he suddenly found himself driving in pouring rain and fifteen miles or so from where he should have been. The car stopped beside a farm gate (as mine had done) and was enveloped in a haze of golden light. (I had experienced complete darkness and the brilliant white circles of light flashing on and off.) The sunshine and dry roads had returned and he continued on his journey, only it had been extended by those extra miles. (In my case natural daylight returned and I then found myself driving in a different part of the village.) Here I was, talking to another person who had experienced many happenings similar to mine. It was a wonderful feeling of relief to speak at last to someone who really knew exactly how I felt.

Graham said that he had the answers to the many questions I must be asking myself, but that it would be a long process for me to gain them as I would have to come to terms with one understanding at a time. These would come gradually and as I learned to accept one, another would begin to become clearer. He said that he did have the answer as to the reasons for the abduction and knew the final outcome but that it would be too much for me to handle all at once.

A feeling of excitement about a new challenge for the future came over me. He said that the information had been revealed to him in dreams and that, in time, it would also be revealed to me. He told me to expect strange things to happen, but would not tell me what and suggested that I should make a note of anything I thought to be unusual. How mysterious it all sounded! I began to realise that what I would now be unravelling would be much more complicated than I had originally expected, but it was comforting to know that there was someone to whom I could turn for an explanation when all these new experiences began to occur.

I was promised a letter setting out the points that had been raised and prepared myself to become involved with another set of unexplained happenings. But – at least this time I did have some warning.

Chapter Thirteen

MY RIGHT TO KNOW

Graham had offered to help me to find the truth about the reason for my abduction, but he explained that to understand all the answers would depend on the right I had earned through my own search. "As," he had said, "answers without understanding are hollow."

My own search. I considered how much effort I had put into it so far. I had tried to find out as much as I could when it had originally happened and up to the time of the hypnosis, then I had gone through a stage of bewilderment because I had not been able to understand the even stranger things that had happened when I had been regressed. Also fear had then become a part of it so I had tried shut it all out. I had put it behind me and had made a great effort to forget that it had ever happened.

Then it had all been resurrected by that phone call from Jenny Randles in 1987 when she was writing her book, *Abduction*. After its publication and Terri's sighting, I found myself becoming curious again. I had read the book carefully with the aim of finding someone I could talk to who had had an encounter similar to mine. It was at that time that I began to feel the need to find someone who could understand what I had been through. I felt that the ridicule, if any, that I would meet this time would be no problem. I had coped with quite a lot in the past. I was now ten years older. I had retired from my teaching career, albeit through ill-health, and had started a new chapter in my life. Here came a new challenge – but at that time only in my mind.

By this time I had been interviewed on Radio Leicester, Wales, Northampton and Bedfordshire and had taken part in Kilroy on BBC1, The Time – The Place on Central TV and This Morning on Granada Television. My close encounter had also been featured in the BUFORA Journal, *She* magazine and in local newspapers, the *Chronicle and Echo*, the *Daventry Weekly Express* and maybe others further afield.

People all over the country had had the opportunity in one way or another to become familiar with my story, but until the actual television appeal no-one had been able to offer any help. Everyone was like me, hoping that an answer would eventually come, but from where? I think, if I am honest, I rather expected to meet my 'UFO Beings' again and be given the answers. I certainly did not expect to have to work at it.

After abductions some people do develop more psychic powers and I was finding that suggestions were coming into my mind which I was able to include in the radio and television interviews. Perhaps this was beginning to happen to me also.

Graham had told no-one but his family the details of his encounter when it had happened. He had not been hypnotised but had relived the experience in a dream since that day, so he knew exactly what happened. As with my compulsion to mention certain points during an interview, he felt a compulsion at that time to get in touch with other people who had had similar experiences. This, he felt, was his role, just one piece of the jigsaw. We were both using the same word.

He forecast on that day that much was then beginning to happen, a start to a three year period when many people would become involved, memories would be returning to abductees and we would begin to know what it was all about. We were being prepared for what was going to happen in the not too distant future.

The following Saturday NUFORC was to hold its next meeting. Graham expressed an interest and I invited him to join the group. He arrived before Joan and I and it was he who welcomed us rather than the other way round. There was a good attendance at the meeting and he related his story, finding as I had done that the many questions which followed were put by people who were also searching to understand some of the reasons for their own encounters.

Looking back, that was the point at which my brother Ted and his wife Janice had come again into the picture. They had maintained an interest in my UFO experience since day one when I had asked their advice and Ted had made those two suggestions. One was to send a copy of my report to R. L. Pearcy, the brother of his colleague during his time in the RAF and who happened to be a member of BUFORA. The other was to inform the Ministry of Defence.

About twelve months prior to this meeting another BUFORA investigator had contacted me for an interview. With my permission he brought along two others with him and I expected and subsequently got a very thorough examination of my case. The idea behind this was to be a book written by him about abduction cases, mine being one which was to be included. Unfortunately, although every word was recorded, the tapes were lost in the post and nothing came of it.

Just after receiving Graham's telephone call I had received another one along the same lines from someone else wishing to use the details of my encounter in an article he was to write for a Sunday newspaper or a Women's magazine. My answer to all these people is always in agreement on one condition – that I am given a copy of the article if it is published, to add to the growing contents of my UFO scrapbook.

My sister-in-law had phoned me on this particular day and knowing of her continuing interest in the subject I had told her about the proposed articles.

"Why don't you write the articles yourself?" she asked. "After all, when women buy women's magazines they expect to read a woman's opinion of the subject, not a man's version of what he thinks she said." Food for thought indeed, and it was following this chat that I decided to write an account myself of the whole experience and the way in which it seemed to be changing my life.

I am sure that UFO activity will increase in the future and that we shall develop a much greater understanding of the reasons for it and as my grand-daughter Terri had also been involved, it seemed to be a good idea to record this aspect of our family history for the benefit of future generations of the Oakensen family. Then, if at some time in the future it should be published, others who have had a similar experience would find points to which they could relate and would find relief and comfort from the fact that they are not alone – as I had felt when first talking to Graham.

This, I knew would be a vast undertaking and possibly would not have a definite ending. It would certainly be a new interest in my retirement and would hopefully keep my mind active and my fingers free from arthritis. I discussed it with the family, friends and members at the NUFORC meeting. The response from all was overwhelming, so much interest I had not really envisaged. But the reason for Graham's enthusiasm was from a different angle entirely. He said that he had no doubt at all that through this writing my understanding would grow.

With each sentence I write I search deeply into my memory and from contact which I have had with others interested in UFOs, those who have been abducted or have had sightings, those I have met on television or radio and people who have contacted me from all over the country, I find the information given to me really does lead to a deeper understanding of, and the coming to terms with, what could be a sensational happening in the future.

Was this, I wondered, what he had meant when he said that to understand all the answers depends on the right which I will have earned through my own search? Would this exercise be deep enough for that understanding to be complete?

Chapter Fourteen

MEDIA PARTICIPATION

In my search for that deeper understanding I was helped by the state of calmness in which I then found myself and by the opportunity to participate with Jenny and other investigators on radio and television programmes. It was a time when I felt at ease and able to answer all the questions put to me when interviewed.

* * *

Repeatedly sitting on a chair in a room in front of a microphone and relating the details of the same story must sound like a very monotonous exercise in whichever building that room happens to be situated, but in fact the experiences I have had when taking part in radio programmes have shown me how varied they can be.

My first experience of this was on a Radio Leicester programme – Chapter five – and this was a situation where John Barden and I sat in a studio at a table to which was attached a microphone. We each described what we had for breakfast so that the engineers could determine the degrees of sound and tone which would give a good reception for the listening public and the interview by Morgan Cross continued from there. The programme was broadcast live to an audience living in Leicestershire and the surrounding counties.

About five years later Radio Northampton was born and each broadcast I have made on that wavelength has been different. The first I described in Chapter six when an interview took place at my home and was followed by visiting the scenes of the action and recording interviews at each relevant stage. These were then broadcast over the air on the following morning, with appropriate music selected by

Nick Herbert being played between each interview.

The second broadcast was a three-way one and I was asked to play my part in Radio Northampton's Daventry Studio whilst Ernest Still was to make his contribution from their studio in Corby. There was a detached feeling about this kind of exercise. The only contact with Northampton was by telephone and I described it later as my 'do-it-yourself' broadcast.

The studio was situated at the top of a building in the High Street, the one used by the Job Centre. I was admitted by one of their staff then left to read the instructions which described how to make contact with the radio station at Northampton. I read the instructions carefully, followed them precisely and 'Hey Presto!' a voice answered. I turned a knob to check voice level and all was set to begin. After a long wait, while I presumed they were contacting Ernest, I was introduced and asked to tell my story.

Following that there were some questions which I answered to clarify a few points, then Ernest was introduced and gave an account of some of the research he had done over the years and a mention too of our newly-formed group NUFORC. Immediately after this we were both thanked, given instructions on how to close down the line and I was told to make sure I locked the door when I left the room.

It had been an interesting experience but, I thought, with rather an abrupt ending. The presenter had asked listeners to 'phone in on a "Dip Poll"' to say whether or not they believed in UFOs and there was no way in which we, who had played such a big part in the programme, could know the result, as there was no way we could reach our homes before it ended. At that time I had no radio in my car and Ernest always travels by public transport.

However, as it happened all was not lost. On arriving home I found that John had been listening to the whole programme and that 100% of the people who had phoned in had said that they believed in UFOs. But I was disappointed to hear that there had been calls from members of the public who had described sightings they had had themselves and would have liked answers to the questions they had been left with afterwards. Had Ernest and I been allowed to stay in our respective studios until the end of the programme, I know we would have been able to pass on more knowledge to the listeners.

My next experience was similar in one way to the last but this time it was at Radio Northampton's own building in Abington Street. It was

97

another link-up, another three-way one, but with other parts of the British Isles instead of just within the same county. I was in Northampton, Jenny Randles was in a studio in Manchester and the programme this time was being broadcast to listeners in Wales. We were being interviewed by Frank Hennesey on his 'Street Life' programme – Chapter eight.

I had twice previously been interviewed along a telephone line and the fifth time I was contacted was for the same reason, in the same way, yet it was entirely different.

On 13th April 1989 I was to be interviewed by telephone from the World Service studio in London whilst I sat at home. This was to be for a programme which was to be relayed in the 'Postmark Africa' series where listeners send in questions on any subject, and answers when researched form part of future programmes.

On this occasion two questions on UFOs had been received from listeners in Nigeria and the researcher felt the programme would be enhanced by a contribution from someone who had experienced an abduction. I was the one chosen.

It was a most interesting half an hour. Firstly the sound levels had to be checked, then I was asked to tell my story. This I started to do, but having explained it so many times I had forgotten that, whilst it had become a logical sequence of events to me, others who had not heard it before would find it hard to understand. I found the interview was very much of a 'stop-start and repeat' nature. At times I seemed to lose the thread of what I was saying, but of course it was most important that the interviewer should comprehend it all and she assured me in the end that she did.

I remarked that it seemed very disjointed to me but Tanya Sillem, who recorded it, said she was very pleased with it and that it would be a very good introduction to the programme which had been devised for that African audience. I assumed that it would be edited and would eventually flow quite smoothly.

I did not catch the name of the UFO expert who was to answer the questions and knew that I would not be able to hear its presentation in the early hours of the morning about a week later, but it was exhilarating to know that the details of my experience, already reported in Europe and the USA, would now reach an audience in another continent.

The most luxurious of all the radio interviews in which I have been involved followed a request from Radio Ulster. It was for an early morning broadcast and I remarked that I was not usually up at that time of the day.

"Don't worry about that," was the cheerful reply, "most of our interviews are done with people in bed, or with people who have a telephone in the shower."

Obviously another of the advantages of radio where only the voice of a person is required. So I did that interview – lying comfortably in bed!

* * *

Around this time I had received another invitation to join Jenny on television. This time it was with Derek Jameson on his programme 'Jameson Tonight' on Sky Television.

The set was not like any other I had seen. We were in the Old Windmill Theatre and it was the nearest I shall ever get to performing on that stage. In semi-darkness, travelling along the corridors and stairs we could sense the atmosphere of days gone by. Jenny had met Derek Jameson before and I felt very much at ease in his company – then I blotted my copybook. I caught sight of myself on a monitor and completely lost the thread of what I was saying, so I had to start again. Fortunately it was being recorded and later that piece was cut out – but I felt so silly at the time.

As our television set at home could not receive Sky TV, I did not expect to see the programme which went out later that evening, but we had friends who did and they very kindly copied it for us. It was the first time I had seen my name with Jenny's in the credits at the end of a programme.

My next visit to a television studio in 1989 was for an entirely different reason. It was to TVS at Southampton where, along with two 'imposters' I had to say, "My name is Elsie Oakensen and I've had a Close Encounter of the Fourth Kind." After briefing Angela Marsh and Anne Edwards for this part of the 'Tell the Truth' programme, rehearsals took place, firstly between the teams of contestants and then, after lunch, with the researchers and studio staff taking the place of the celebrity team and the chairman.

The two imposters from each of the two groups making up the one programme took part in the second half of the show. This was when they tried to fool the team individually. One held a record or was famous for some reason in his or her own right and the other three had to speak for a short-time describing something at which they professed to excel equally well.

On this occasion one of the four had gained sixteen 'A' level passes in the GCE examinations and the other three had to convince their opposite number in the celebrity team that he or she had sixteen of something as well. It was great fun helping them to decide what to have. Everyone in the studio made suggestions and eventually it was decided that Angela should have sixteen brothers, whilst Anne's cat was to have had sixteen kittens. Angela was from a large family and found it quite easy to reel off sixteen men's names, and the records were consulted to find that a cat had actually had fifteen kittens so sixteen would indeed be a record.

The celebrity panel for our game consisted of Leslie Crowther, Jenny Leigh-Wright, Peter Woods and Alison Holloway.

The signed statement read by the chairman to the panel said, 'I Elsie Oakensen had an encounter with extraterrestrial beings ten years ago. I was driving home from work one winter evening when I saw two lights emanating from a strange object in front of me. My car began to lose power and eventually stopped. It was completely dark. Then strange circles of white light began to flash on and off. The next thing I knew it was fifteen minutes later and I was travelling down the road in a different part of the village. I am convinced I was selected by aliens earlier in the day and later rejected. Signed: Elsie Oakensen.'

"But which is the real Elsie Oakensen?" he asked them. "Number one, two or three?" The panel had to decide but there were two jokers there, two impostors in the pack who would do their best to deceive the panel. Angela and Anne were very determined ladies.

In turn the celebrities fired questions for the allotted time at each of us. I, as 'Elsie One', had to explain to Allison Holloway what had happened to me whilst the car had stopped and Angela, as 'Elsie Two', told why she was not frightened. She said that it appeared to her that they had calmed her when they first selected her earlier in the day. "Why had they selected you?" was the next question.

"Well, no-one can explain that to me. I wish I knew," she answered calmly.

Peter Woods obviously felt that he was not going to be taken in by us and raised a laugh when he asked 'Elsie Three' if she could please tell everyone the name of the public house she had been visiting just before this had happened. Anne answered seriously that she had not been drinking as she was on her way home from work. He thought there might have been an office party, and he then questioned Angela and me about any psychic interests we might have, then Anne again to ascertain whether or not the car had required attention at a garage afterwards.

Jenny Leigh-Wright thought it was a fascinating statement and said that she found it very hard to believe, then she furthered Alison's line of questioning by asking me whether or not I was asleep whilst I sat in the car and how, when fifteen minutes had elapsed and I found myself travelling down the road, did I think I had got there?

I said I had no idea at all – it was if it all happened by remote control. She had to be assured that I was not dreaming. Then Angela was asked what time she arrived home that evening and that completed that panel member's questioning time.

Leslie Crowther wanted to know the time of the year and about weather conditions and whether Angela often had blackouts when she was driving her car! Anne was asked the name of the village where her encounter had taken placed and answered "Marchwood". Then he asked me where it had been. "Was it Marchwood and where was Marchwood?" We had been advised that if that question was asked we should each name a village we knew well so that our answers would sound convincing and there was always the chance that if we were all asked the same question and each gave a different answer it would confuse the panel.

But my answers had to be truthful and anyway everyone loves to hear the name of their own village mentioned on the television or radio. So I replied truthfully that my experience was in Church Stowe in Northamptonshire. He then asked me if I had told lots of people about it and what was their reaction. He seemed surprised when I said, "A bit cynical and very rude in some cases."

That ended the allocated time for questioning us and the time had come for the panel to decide which Elsie was telling the truth.

Both Angela and Anne were hoping that no-one would guess it really was me.

Alison thought it was Angela because she was rather quiet about it. She said that there was something in her eyes which made her think that she might have had an experience of that sort and she added that if we had had that sort of experience she felt very sorry for us as she would have been terrified.

Peter thought that it seemed a long way for me to have come to tell them about my experience if it had happened in Northamptonshire, so he chose Anne because he felt that she seemed as though she could have had that kind of experience.

Jenny was not convinced it was Anne and she thought that with Angela it could not have been possible, but she decided it was me because I had immediately said the name of the village after Anne had named another one and that I was absolutely sure of where it was.

Leslie thought it was very difficult to know which sort of person would actually have an experience such as this and although he thought Angela had a 'visionary' look he eventually decided to give his vote to Anne. So that meant I had one vote, Angela had one and Anne had two. We had beaten three of the four members of the panel.

Then the pressure was taken off when the chairman said, "Will the real Elsie Oakensen stand up please?" and of course I did. It was quite something to see the expressions on their faces. The audience applauded. Jenny was congratulated on her success and Angela and Anne were praised for being two marvellous impostors. They were then introduced in their own right as Angela Marsh, a relief manager, and Anne Edwards, a journalist.

Then, as the 'Real Elsie Oakensen' I faced questions from the chairman and members of the panel. Did this actually happen? Did you actually see the aliens? Do you think they intended to harm you? Were they evil or were they not? Why do you think they rejected you? Has it happened again? Have you had any other visions or dreams?

The final question, from the chairman, was whether some people think I am mad. "Oh yes, quite a lot of people do," I replied. Then he assured me that I had just experienced the next worst thing to that – 'Tell the Truth' – and he thanked me for joining them.

The next part of the programme was the one-to-one session and the chairman introduced it by saying that the one thing the panel did not know about the four previous impostors was that one of them had sixteen of something which he was happy to have two of – which caused roars of laughter. Each member of the panel questioned the person opposite and Leslie was right in not believing that Anne's cat had sixteen kittens, whilst Jenny was wrong in believing that Angela could have sixteen brothers. The person who actually did have sixteen 'A' level passes was Francis Thomason who also had seventy 'O' level passes in different subjects and is mentioned in the *Guinness Book of Records*.

After our programme had been recorded we sat in the audience during the recording of the next one, then all participants and their relatives joined the celebrity panel and the television staff at a reception in another part of the building. There I met Anne's family too and later Angela and her family drove me back to the hotel for a final chat about UFOs before my return home the following morning.

* * *

Because of the inclusion of my story in Jenny Randle's book I had then made four appearances on television, three of those to support her in the promotion of that book, there had been radio interviews too and I was learning what demands there are on an author after publication. Jenny had certainly worked hard to bring *Abduction* to the notice of the public and I was glad to have helped.

Up to that point my initiation into the world of the media had taught me many things, amongst them that the subject with which I was becoming more involved could easily be sensationalised, therefore I was exposed to ridicule and sarcasm from a far greater audience. Newspapers and magazines were no exception. The local ones were very understanding but further afield the reporters and headline writers seemed to need something eye-catching to sell their products and more outrageous they became as those writing the headlines chose the word 'aliens' to draw in the readers. According to them, not only was I "Kidnapped by an Alien from Outer Space", but I had also been "Hijacked by an Alien Spacecraft" and "Hunted by a UFO" – all of which John and I found very amusing. To cope with this I learned that I must come across as being genuine, honestly admitting if I did not understand something or why these things had happened. I also had to put myself in the place of the interviewer and understand that it was equally necessary for him or her to put the sceptics' view forward for comment as well.

Of course, newspaper reports have to be accompanied by a photograph and this can be quite an experience too. Usually the session follows a telephone interview with the reporter who requires it to accompany his article.

"It won't take long. Just a photograph of you with your car at appropriate places along the route," I am told, and although I point out that it is not the same car (it was then a white Renault 5 but is now a red

Volvo), it doesn't seem to matter – a car is a car. It sounds so simple, but an hour and a half and three rolls of film later, I feel quite bedraggled and am very pleased that I am not a photographic model.

A photograph in my home is not as simple as it sounds either. I have stood by the window for what seems like an eternity being positioned so that the outside light on one side of my face supplements that from the flashlight on the other side. I have to look pensive, inquisitive, worried – very rarely happy. I have yet to convince a photographer that I really was fascinated by the whole experience and not at all afraid.

One photographer required photographs from above. For what reason I never did understand. Perhaps he had always wanted to travel in a UFO and see an "alien's" view of earthly beings. We had to find a ladder for him and I was asked to look heavenwards. That caused a problem too as no-one had explained to him that ageing citizens often have cataracts which cause the light to scatter in their eyes, also that the glare of a large expanse of sky, even on a dull day can cause one to squint.

Even so, what starts as a serious but 'fun' session usually finds the photographer having to considerably alter his preconceived ideas and on that occasion it was decided that I should climb the ladder and that he would photograph a worm's-eye view. I didn't like to tell him that I had no head for heights either!

Usually a photographer who appears separately will listen to my story first and I'll take him along the route so that he can decide which aspects of the sighting he wishes to portray.

The farm gate was the point where the most dramatic episode happened, but that is in the centre of Church Stowe. One photographer came with the preconceived idea that being in the countryside meant panoramic views everywhere, so on that occasion we had to find gateways which obliged. His instructions had been to photograph me and the car and each of the photographs did just that from all angles, all with a very scenic background.

Another young man was not aware that elderly ladies who are asked to stoop down for a photograph may not be able to rise again without help. I explained that I was "a bit arthriticky" and that although I would comply with his request I may need some help to get up again. Often when sitting on a soft chair I need help too and John will always oblige. He usually stands up in front of me and offers me his hand which I grip. Then he, being of large stature, stands solidly whilst I pull myself up to standing position. The photographer was short and very slim but offered me his hand. His reaction on my coming up from ground level was one of complete surprise and he lost his balance. A complete rethink of methods quickly became necessary.

Another time the car had been manoeuvred into the correct position and I was asked to lean against the front mudguard, very like the models at the Motor Show. It was a very blustery day and my hairdo had already been ruined.

The posture required of me on this occasion was for me to look heavenward with both arms outstretched and a look of surprise on my face. The photographer looked through the viewer on his camera. My stance was satisfactory. As I stretched out my arms into position, had he taken a snap at that point there certainly would have been a look of astonishment on my face. A strong gust of wind blew my skirt high into the air. "We don't want a Marilyn Monroe look," he said seriously, so only one arm was able to be outstretched whilst the other held down my skirt.

But the most confusion comes when a visiting reporter has already heard my story and has decided on the type of photograph he would like to accompany his article, then the photographer appears on the scene having been delayed at a previous assignment. The two invariably have completely different ideas as to the content of the required photograph. I feel really sorry for the reporter under these circumstances as he must have a terrible job finding one which is appropriate to illustrate the points which he wants to get across in his article.

All this I have taken in my stride and if I am honest I have enjoyed every moment of it. Different aspects of the media have opened up for me and it was interesting each time to see the different ways in which behind-the-scenes operations were put into action.

If that close encounter nearly eleven years before had occurred so that I could spread the word about UFOs, for whatever reason at sometime in the future, then all these dealings with the media were a good training ground.

During that euphoric six months I was able to answer questions calmly and outwardly show that I was trying to be objective and had an understanding of everyone else's point of view about the subject. This was also increasing my confidence to cope with whatever might lay ahead.

Chapter Fifteen

ICUR

Life sailed along very smoothly and I looked forward to the International Congress for UFO Research. I have always enjoyed attending conferences, especially when I have not been giving a lecture. Every one who attends is there because of an interest in the subject, which makes for a very pleasant atmosphere. Points are raised and opinions expressed providing a setting in which more balanced conclusions can be reached.

I had not attended anything on UFOs which lasted longer than the NUFORC meetings, so to have three whole days being involved with a conference on that very subject, especially as it was entitled 'Abduction', was right up my street.

I had still only met Graham who had had a similar experience and an added attraction was the possibility that I might meet others there.

The official opening of the conference was timetabled for 10.30 a.m. on 14th July 1989 with an address by the President of BUFORA, Sir Patrick Wall, MC, VRD, RM (Ret) and the afternoon programme was to be a debate on abduction.

Before the proceedings began, Jenny had given everyone a questionnaire and two of the questions were, 'Have you seen a UFO?' and 'Have you had a time lapse?' Introducing part one of the debate, Jenny had given the results of these and I found that there were three people present who were abductees. I hoped that before I went home I would meet the other two. How, I did not know, as it is not everyone who is willing to talk openly about such an experience.

Speakers presenting their views on this subject as an introduction to the debate were John Spencer, Walter H. Andrews Jr. (USA), Maurizio Verga (Italy), Cynthia Hind (South Africa) and Claude Mauge (France).

Audience participation was welcomed in the second part of the debate

106

and it covered many things in relation to the investigations of abductees, such as what type of person should do the investigation, also the pros and cons of regressive hypnosis and it was during this section that I felt I could contribute something worthwhile.

Having made contact with Graham, and experiencing through that a feeling of support and understanding for which I had waited so long, I was able to voice an opinion on 'Support Groups for Abductees'. Also, while I had the microphone I was able to relate my experience of 'On-site Visualisation', a subject which had been mentioned earlier but with no explanation. I described my journey along the route of my encounter with Nick Herbert from Radio Northampton (Chapter six) and explained how helpful it had been when doing that experiment for Jenny to use when writing her book.

From that point I was no longer an ordinary member of the group. I had gone 'public' and everyone wanted to hear the details. So interested were they that in every spare moment, coffee, lunch, tea breaks and even during the gala dinner, I was asked to relate what had happened. Sir Patrick also wanted to know and on the final day a slot was found and I was timetabled to give an account of my experience to the whole assembly.

Towards the end of the first day, fifteen people formed an 'Abduction Panel' and spent the time discussing mainly what clues could be looked for in deciding whether a case is an abduction or not. The point was also raised that perhaps abductees would be the best people to investigate other abductees. I did not feel happy about that. I was sure that I would not have the confidence to do it but did not say so at the time as I felt it needed further thought on my part.

The following day everything seemed clearer to me and I was prepared to submit the following points to the next meeting of the panel.

1. No, I did not feel that an abductee should investigate another abductee, but support and counsel – yes.

2. I felt that other investigations should be carried out by people who could be objective and who could put the feet of the person who had the sighting firmly back on the ground.

3. An investigator should be able, if it was needed (and I did) to give a telephone number or the name of a person who had been in a similar position (with that person's consent, of course) to the witness whose sighting was being investigated, so that contact could be made and support be given. I had waited ten and a half years for this and I was

lucky to have been able to make my own appeal on television. Very few would have that opportunity. The peace of mind that I had received in the knowledge that I could now contact someone going through a similar experience was indescribable.

During the afternoon I also took part in an Anamnesis Survey which Ken Phillips was conducting. This means 'life memory' and consisted of sixty-four questions which I answered giving details of my life from birth to that day, also of the encounter. When completed it would be sent to Dr. Alex Keul of Salzburg University in Austria, where it would be collated with others to see if there is a common thread to enable a decision to be made as to what type of person becomes an abductee.

The gala dinner that evening turned out to be something unexpected, a bit like a Close Encounter! The first course was already on the plate. It was a variety of fruits with prawns and a sauce – all in the shape of a spaceship. Much thought had obviously gone into the menu which read: Apollo Turkey Capsule, Space Balls, Green Fingers and Martian Mallow Cream. I enjoyed the meal and the company very much and the topic of conversation throughout was UFOs – of course!

When eventually I went to bed at midnight I realised that I had described my encounter four times that day to different groups of people, but that was not the thing that astonished me most. Immediately after the part of the debate in which I had spoken, one of the other two abductees had made herself known to me, but only for a moment and then she was gone. Then a couple had spoken to me.

"We knew you were someone special when you came into the room," the lady said. "We saw your aura."

"I didn't know I had one," I answered feebly, but they wanted to make sure they heard my story before they left and I was not able to pursue it further. This aura was something I would have to look into after I arrived home.

On the second day my CE4 (Close Encounter of the Fourth Kind), as it was now being referred to, still commanded interest. Tony was a visitor from Sweden who wanted me to talk to him about it. He borrowed Malcolm Robinson's tape recorder and asked if we could record an interview on tape. He said he had never met an abductee before and wanted to take back the voice as well as the story.

That day Bertil Kuhleman from Sweden assured us that UFO activity would increase over the next year. I had heard Ernest and Graham forecast that too. It was suggested that whirlwinds or vortices might be responsible for corn circles and that hoax circles could easily be detected because the corn is broken and the ears are damaged whereas in the genuine ones the corn lies flat and there are two or three circles of corn usually bent over in different directions. The corn in these continued to grow.

Cynthia Hind talked about "Close Encounter Effects on People in Africa". This was most interesting and we heard about one black African who had a voice in his head telling him to make a machine. This was subsequently done and is now used in mines on that continent. It reminded me of Graham's experience and the fact that he had received similar information.

Walt Andrews gave a slide presentation on the "Gulf Breeze Photographic Case" but the evidence was disputed by Wally Smith who had sent a paper claiming that it was all a hoax. This was discussed at length.

The fault of all conferences which I have attended is that there is always too little time to fit in everything which arises from 'day one'. It was the same at this one. Everything over-ran its time and the abduction debate was eventually cancelled so I was not able to present the points which I had formulated to the rest of the Abduction Panel.

Lionel Beer who is a founder member of BUFORA, is also a specialist bookseller and had on the first evening presented a light-hearted view of UFOs illustrated by cartoons in his role as an after dinner speaker. It was most enjoyable and raised many a laugh.

He was in charge of the book shop and there I was able to find everything I had not been able to buy nearer home. The *Scoriton Mystery* which Gary H. had suggested I should read, also *Communion* which Graham had recommended.

The film show on the second night had included *The UFO Experience* about UFO investigation in the USA, the *Police Video Incident* (the hypnosis of an abductee) and two films about Corn Circles. It was a very interesting hour and a half.

The third day started with UFO News Updates and Ken Phillips reported on his Anamnesis Research Project. Then, though time was at a premium, I was given ten minutes to describe my close encounter so that by the time the congress ended everyone present had heard it. Afterwards I was asked by the representatives of several organisations to write an article for their magazines and felt very honoured.

Having joined John Spencer on Radio Bedfordshire it was interesting to hear him speak at length on 'Witness-driven investigations'. I am sure that it is sometimes difficult for investigators to be as objective as they ought to be and witnesses are led on occasions to feel that they should answer in a certain way – I remembered that feeling myself. John felt that the impetus for the investigations should come from the witnesses themselves. It was they who should lead the investigation in whichever way they felt to be the right one. This would mean that it would be their perception of whatever they thought had happened. He felt that more varied stories and perhaps less coherent ones would come from this but it would provide a clearer understanding of what actually happened.

I had heard much emphasis on the contamination of witnesses in the various speeches. My own hypnosis session had been inconclusive. I wished by then that I had had another session, but now I knew too much about UFOs and I was in this class described as 'contaminated'. Jenny's experiment which I had carried out had been a kind of self-hypnosis but not a lot had come from that. Perhaps I was too afraid to dig too deeply. Neither Jenny nor John felt that another session of hypnosis would be right for me now and suggested that I should think about meditation if I felt there was really more to know. This was something else to look into later.

Jenny reported on the Abduction Panel's findings and listed twelve points which the panel recommended should be taken into consideration when having to decide whether or not a Close Encounter is an Abduction.

After the congress had finished I met Malcolm Robinson who is the Editor of the *Journal of Strange Phenomena Investigations.* It reminded me of the cover of the *Strange Phenomena Publication* which I had been given by its Editor, Graham Phillips, and its Senior Research Co-ordinator, Andy Collins, on the day during which they and Martin Keatman had spent the afternoon with John and me when I had been hypnotised. They were known to Malcolm and it was good to have news of them after such a long time.

Then Malcolm introduced me to Mary and my wish from day one when Jenny had given me the results of her questionnaire had come true. Mary was the third abductee present. We found that we had much in common, even to travelling home from the same London station and we hoped that sometime in the future we may both meet again.

During those three days I had heard about UFO research in Sweden, France, Italy, Africa and the USA as well as Britain and I had met many people who before had just been names. It was a very good initiation into a more thorough understanding of the UFO phenomenon.

It was also leading to a deeper interest in many other things which seemed to be connected with my encounter. Now I had to find out about my aura and I would also need to come to terms with the possibility that meditation could provide a contact with those 'beings' which I had described as ghost-like and which Jenny said could be interpreted as 'people'.

I seemed to have stopped asking questions and appeared to be at a point where new aspects needed to be investigated.

Chapter Sixteen

CHANGING COURSE

A copy of BUFORA's lecture programme for 1989/90 had been sent to me by Philip Mantle and among the regional lectures arranged was one to be held in Northampton on 20th January 1990 when members of the NUFORC group would be the hosts to visitors from all parts of the country. Ernest Still was scheduled to discuss 'Northamptonshire UFO Cases' and Steve Gamble to do an 'Analysis of Photographic Cases'.

Among the visitors were four people I had met at the ICUR conference in London the previous July and, following an account which I gave of my sighting during Ernest's lecture, questions put to me by Roy made me realise that the time had come to analyse the suggestions, thoughts and comments which I had collected up to that point. This was also endorsed when a complete stranger asked, "Why do you want answers anyway? That is all in the past you know. And why do you think you were rejected? You were not, you know."

Feelings that I was becoming backward thinking instead of looking forward came flooding into my mind and it became obvious that, although I was looking for answers to help me understand what had happened during that encounter, the place I would be most likely to find an answer to the question, "Why me?" lay directly in the future.

I decided then to summarise my findings to date, assess the situation at that point and rethink my technique.

• When I turned at the traffic lights and saw the red and green lights attached to that dark shape above the A5, my immediate thought had been that it was an aircraft which would zoom over my head and because of its height I felt certain that it would crash some distance behind me.

112

- Red and green lights are landing lights on a plane and I could be forgiven for taking them as such at that time, but Roy pointed out that a red light is on the port (left) side of a plane and the green light on the starboard (right) side. If it had been a plane I would have seen it fly over the crossroads in front of me as I approached the traffic lights and as I turned there it would have been flying in front of me and travelling in the same direction as I was. Perhaps I should have known that and the UFO's lights were purposely the other way round to ensure that I would not confuse it with a normal aircraft and would then look at it with interest.
- When I reached the top of the hill and looked back, I was then level with the UFO, seeing a side view of it. When the green light started to flash, I treated that as a signal, probably: "Here we come – we'll stop the car at the next corner."
- On turning at the T-junction the electrics of the car were interfered with but the car did not come to a complete halt. I think I was too near a covering of trees for that to happen.
- Many people, including Roy, have asked me whether the car functioned normally afterwards. It did, in fact the side-light bulb which was not functioning before the encounter, worked normally afterwards and never needed replacing.
- The display of flashing lights, I believe, was to keep my human mind occupied whilst perhaps other things were happening to my body. A medical examination had been suggested. Maybe – especially if the light which came towards me (under hypnosis) was an X-ray, and if my 'ghost-like beings' really were aliens, extraterrestrials, or could be interpreted by the human mind as 'people'.
- Realisation after this was that the natural light had returned and that I was in a position further along the road in exactly the same gear and travelling at exactly the same speed as when I had reached the end of the tree-covered part of the road.
- How had I got there? I had certainly not driven myself along that part of the road. I believe the 'remote' control I originally described it as being, was in fact 'UFO control'.
- On arrival at home I found that my journey had taken fifteen minutes longer than it should have done. What was I doing during that time? Obviously sitting in my car being manipulated by those beings.
- The yellow flashing light I saw from the bedroom window I am sure

113

now was all part of the illusion, probably signalling 'mission accomplished'.

- The tightening sensations around my head, one at lunch time and one in the evening, also the same thing under hypnosis: all three were linked to the same experience, I was sure.

It was suggested that at lunch time it was a contact from the occupants of the UFO tuning in to my subconscious mind to tell me that I had been selected for closer inspection during my journey home and to assure me that I would not be afraid. That made sense to me.

I could believe also that the same thing happened as I reached the point where an examination of some kind, not necessarily medical, obviously took place and as more knowledgeable people than I consider that the evening sighting at Preston Capes was a true corroboration of my story, I believe that the UFO was still in the area, perhaps examining evidence that had been collected during my journey home and that was 'their' way during the evening of letting me know that they were satisfied with their findings.

This time I was not even considering the word 'rejection'.

During 1988 many people made contact with me after seeing me on a television programme or hearing me in a radio interview – also because my name and telephone number were being passed on by investigators who knew that I was anxious to share my experience with anyone who would understand, or who perhaps needed to talk to someone themselves about a similar experience they had had.

On most occasions I was asked whether I thought of my 'aliens' as being friendly, to which I have always answered, 'Yes.' But gradually it became more obvious that I was speaking to and later meeting people like Graham who were more aware of what was happening because of their own contact with these entities.

I was being told that I had a role to play in the future as all abductees had, but no-one could tell me what. "It will become clearer in time," I was assured. A new kind of interest in the reason for UFOs was beginning and I began to be asked to speak openly about everything to groups of people in a variety of situations, this time in a setting where questions of all types needing immediate answers could be fired at me – a very challenging situation indeed and one which needed a very confident manner to convince the questioner that the subject of UFOs and the information which I had given them was in fact genuine.

Chapter Seventeen

MY ROLE?

An article I once read explained how we are prepared over a period of time for an event which will take place in the future. I do believe our lives are mapped out for us but it is not until we have achieved something of which we are particularly proud that we look back and work through the route of preparation for that assignment.

I have also always believed that that close encounter in 1978 was for a purpose, that there was some reason behind it, but what? After all this time I could still only guess. I sometimes wished I had had a second session of regressive hypnosis. Perhaps then I might have known to expect a change in my way of life when *Abduction* was published and I found myself on radio broadcasts and television programmes with Jenny.

I am sure that book was a medium through which my interest in UFOs was rekindled. Appearing on the media I was to find that, ten years later, the UFO phenomenon was becoming more acceptable to the public, that I would meet other abductees with whom I could share experiences and that I would have opportunities to share my opinions with the world, expressing thoughts which were beginning to flow into my mind.

Incidents began to happen which made me feel that perhaps my role would be in the way of publicity or communication, after all I was talking freely about the encounter and the hypnosis and people were taking me seriously, realising that my story had never changed. They were believing now that it really had happened and that it was not a hoax.

When Jenny told me that she wished to include an account of my experience in her book I had asked her what had made my sighting so special. She answered that it was my 'normality'. Apparently a lot of people read books, then fantasise about their own experiences, but I just stated facts. Maybe that was an influence from other members of the family. After all, the police are only interested in facts and John, our eldest son Derek and his wife Christine were all members of the force. Perhaps some of this had rubbed off on me!

Whilst taking part in television appearances and radio broadcasts, also the contact with NUFORC members and regular attendances at their meetings, my fund of knowledge regarding UFOs was increasing steadily, and without my realising it, was becoming a genuine interest in my retirement.

Then, whilst looking back at a series of incidents which had taken place over many months during 1988 and 1989 I came to deduce that there could perhaps be this particular purpose for it all after all.

* * *

Mona Cross is a Quaker friend of mine who can always see the best in a person and, notwithstanding being in her eighties, is always ready to help anyone no matter what inconvenience is caused to herself whilst doing so. She is a lovely lady from whom I have learned much about human nature.

One of her hobbies is painting and each year she has been on a trip to paint scenery in France, Belgium or even a holiday visit to relatives in Canada. She attends classes locally and it is a great pleasure for her to join a weekend or even a week's course in a college for adult education.

Her interests lie not only in painting, because as an ex-headmistress she followed her former pupils' interests as she watched them develop. This caring relationship is also extended to her friends and I consider myself to be greatly honoured to be one of them. So, as with all her protégés, she tried to understand my interest in UFOs.

During the latter part of 1988 she attended one of her weekend courses and, during conversation with other members there, the subject of UFOs had arisen and this prompted her next phone call to me.

"I've just been on a course at Knuston Hall," she said, "David Clark is looking for someone to talk to members of his group about UFOs and I said I knew someone who knew all about them. Would you be prepared to help him?"

According to her information, David's course 'Explaining the Unexplained' included information about UFOs and he was looking for someone with a personal knowledge of the subject to talk to his group.

Panic set in. Mona liked immediate answers. Whilst I had happily talked to the NUFORC group of which I had not long been a member and where it definitely was a case of preaching to the converted, and to people in the street or supermarkets who had broached the subject because they knew me, at that time it was usually a one to one discussion – an official lecture was something altogether different. Also there was the fact that I always made sure I had a passenger when I drove anywhere other than to do local shopping and I still did not drive anywhere alone after dark.

"Well, I can give you the telephone number of Ernest Still. He would do it," I replied. "He is the Chairman of NUFORC and does a lot of talks. He's also done a lot of research over many years and has many more facts at his fingertips than I have."

Mona was disappointed. She wanted me to do it. She knew my story. She had heard it from me originally and she's heard me tell it on local radio and seen me on television. She was sure I was the right person to help. I was flattered by her faith in me but very unsure of my ability to do it justice at that time.

She took Ernest's telephone number and reluctantly said she would pass it on. I phoned Ernest to explain what I had done and was assured that if contact was made with him he would be happy to go along and give a talk. The subject of formal lecturing to adults was then put firmly to the back of my mind.

*   *   *

About six months later I received a phone call from Jenny Randles. She was going to appear on a children's TV programme and wondered whether I knew of a child who had seen a UFO and who would be willing to be with her on the programme. Well, Terri had seen two the previous October and, after careful counselling from me and investigation by Ernest, was coming to terms with it and was beginning to talk openly about it. At just eleven years of age, Jenny thought she would be just right and, after conversation between Jenny, the TV company and Rose, Terri's mother, it was decided that 'Nannie' should be delegated to take her to the Border TV studios at Carlisle.

There it was extremely interesting for me to see how UFOs were dealt with at a child's level. Care was taken not to frighten the children watching the programme and to ensure that when it was broadcast Terri

117

would not be ridiculed by her school friends.

I had never spoken to children about my sighting and had only given Terri a basic outline of it as I talked to her after her encounter, so it was interesting to see at first hand how the other children there reacted on and off the set during the day and how it was presented during the recording of the programme.

We watched the finally edited programme and the presentation was such that I am sure no children would have been frightened however young they were.

* * *

A few days after this I received a phone call from another friend, Kate Butcher. Kate was a teacher at the Gyosei International School for Japanese children in Milton Keynes. She had been teaching a science lesson to her class when the subject of UFOs arose.

"I have a friend who has seen a UFO," she had told them.

"Will she come and tell us about it?" they asked. Well, I did. I had never driven to Milton Keynes before so Kate sent me a map. All the streets were numbered, a thing I had not noticed on the several occasions I had been shopping with John – until his last visit, a few days before the Carlisle TV recording.

On the appointed day I drove myself there in his vehicle as mine was just about on its last legs and we had not decided then on a replacement for it. I originally expected to be talking to one class of twelve to thirteen-year-olds but finished up talking to two classes of that age and two classes of high school children aged seventeen to eighteen years.

With the younger children I found that the inside knowledge I had gained from the children's TV programme was extremely useful – but the other two groups were adults and more in number than I had ever spoken to before. There was genuine interest from them all irrespective of age and very searching, sensible questions were asked.

During one of the senior group's classes I was suddenly aware that I could talk non-stop on the subject for forty-five minutes and on the way home, driving along the A5, I realised that my confidence had returned when driving alone over distances further than in my own local area.

The following month my ancient Renault Five was replaced by a new second-hand Volvo with twenty-nine miles on the clock and driving really had become a pleasure again. Then on the back of an envelope I found the notes I had made of that original phone call from Mona and I knew that if I were still required I would not hesitate to go along myself and talk to the people on the course.

* * *

On 8th November 1989 that opportunity arose. I was paying my usual visit to Mona when out of the blue she announced that she was going to ring the college to tell the lecturer that I was willing to take part in this course. She did so straight away. I spoke to him and it was arranged that I should join the group for lunch on Saturday 13th January 1990 and speak to them during the afternoon session. This was to be followed by a discussion.

Final arrangements were made a few weeks later and I arrived at Knuston Hall in Northamptonshire, a residential college for Adult Education, on the specified Saturday to join the course members for lunch.

The talk was introduced by David Clark who had a video of a TV programme in which I had appeared, one in which it was considered not enough time was allowed for me to describe my encounter properly and where the interviewer had hurried the story along, causing some viewers to be disappointed.

About three weeks prior to this day, Derrick, Kate Butcher's husband, had accompanied me along the route of that journey with his camera and had taken photographs from various points along the way so that I would have a series of slides to accompany my talk. I had also prepared overhead projector transparancies to use and was armed with a list of important stages which I felt it necessary to mention.

There were about twenty adults in the class, including Mona. I described my close encounter in detail and illustrated it with the slides. I outlined my search for reasons for it and my renewed interest, after a period of nine years, which had led to my involvement with the media. I gave an account of the strange things which were happening to me then and which I could not explain and talked about some of the people I had met who were helping me to find answers. I also mentioned NUFORC and their next meeting to be held the following Saturday and was to find later that three members of the group were interested enough to enquire for details and say that they hoped to be able to come along to it.

During the tea break I noticed a timetable of the course contents in the cloakroom and realised that after I was scheduled to leave, that part of the programme was entitled 'Is there anybody there? UFO phenomena' so I volunteered to stay. It was here I realised that I had talked non-stop for an hour in the first session, so there had been no time for questions. Now came the opportunity and I met with some very searching but understanding queries.

I also heard of experiences which others had had. One man explained that, although he did not see a UFO, he had felt very strange whilst driving along a country road. He stopped and noticed what seemed to be fog with thousands of small lights sparkling through it, causing him to think that it was unwise to stay, so he drove off. Another lady had seen a UFO whilst living in Australia.

I was glad I had stayed on. I found that the interest my talk had aroused was such that every member of the group had a question, an opinion, or a situation to describe which gave me the opportunity to think as well as to listen and to answer.

As the session closed David asked if I would return to take part in the next course later in the year and I accepted his invitation, but the most rewarding time of all was when Mona, who has two hearing aids, said that she had heard what I had said and understood it better now and that it had been a very good afternoon. That made me feel great. I had lived up to her expectation of me.

It was dark when I left Knuston Hall and the temperature had dropped below freezing point. One gentleman escorted me to the car park and insisted on scraping the ice from my car windows. I drove the twenty-six miles home alone. It was the first time I had travelled that distance alone in the dark for at least six years. Another hurdle had been passed.

* * *

It had been suggested to me by then that I was being guided along a certain course in preparation for a purpose which at some time in the future would become clear to me.

The sceptics of course will say, "Well that is life. It is full of new experiences which add to its richness and prepare us for meeting new challenges in the future" – and I agree – but having acomplished a successful feat, when I look back there has always been a pattern to it.

120

Some things which had seemed unimportant at the time in relation to what I was doing, obviously made a mark in my memory and I wondered why. Then later, although they had seemed to have no connection, everything had fitted into place and what had once seemed to be an impossible task had become very possible and I had performed it with such confidence that it surprised me.

Chapter Eighteen

THE PARANORMAL AND UFOS

Where to draw the line between UFOs and the paranormal was a question posed by Gerald Maine when interviewing John Spencer and me on the BBC Radio Bedfordshire programme, but should a line be drawn between them at all? Is the UFO phenomenon not just one aspect of the whole subject?

In order to try and understand whether or not this may be so, I was asked to give an account of my UFO experiences to the participants of a development group which was organised by a friend who was a medium and a spiritual healer, so that a study could be made. It was an extremely interesting evening, though at the time I knew very little about spiritualism and curious rather than interested better described how I felt about it. This meeting took place just after *Abduction* was published and about eighteen months after that I was to become involved in some research which was being carried out by a television company and which would provide me with an answer.

* * *

In October 1989 I heard again from Ken Phillips who I had met at the ICUR Conference (Chapter fifteen). Jane Eames was in the process of researching material for fifteen programmes on the paranormal and one was to be about UFOs. He wondered if I would be willing to be interviewed and I agreed.

The following day Jane rang. She said that she was looking at different aspects of the paranormal and that on each programme there would be three people taking part – one person to describe an experience, one an expert in the investigation of that aspect and one experienced in psychological research. Everything was to be treated seriously and the series would be shown in the early part of 1990.

I related the story of my encounter and heard that others would be interviewed also, that only one would be selected and that recordings would take place in December. I had several more calls regarding the programme. Jane said that she was fascinated by my story and very fairly explained that she was looking into other abductees' accounts as well as mine and that a final selection would be made nearer the recording date. Later I was told that the candidates had been narrowed down to two and that I was one of them. I was asked to keep five dates free in December in case I would be finally selected to take part.

Four of the five dates had passed and I had heard nothing so I assumed that the other person had been chosen. In fact, I would go so far as to say that I knew that I would not be taking part – and this is why. Over the previous year when I had been involved in radio or TV broadcasts I had experienced a sense of calmness prior to the day and I had received some kind of mental communication putting thoughts into my head about points I should raise during the programme. This time it was not happening. I was relatively calm, but tired and a bit headachy and not in an alert enough frame of mind to take part. So, when Jane rang on the 15th I was not at all surprised to hear her say that another lady's story had been chosen instead.

What did surprise me, however, was that she was so impressed with mine, and the account of my sighting that Cicely had typed all those years ago, also newspaper cuttings dated from that time that I had sent to her, that she hoped I would be able to go along as well. She said that Linda's story was a very sensitive one and that because of this she may decide not to take part, so would I go along as a stand-by and replace her if she did not turn up.

The final three recordings were to be done on the 19th December and I could spend the whole day there if I wished. The early one was to be about spiritualism and the final one about dreams. I could watch them all being recorded, all meals would be provided and all expenses paid.

I arrived at the Thames Television Studio in London that day as the first of the programmes was about to be recorded. It was about the spirit world, a subject in which I was then becoming very much more interested. One lady taking part was to give an account of a meeting in the night with her small daughter who had died in an accident.

After the three people who were taking part in the recording had gone to the studio, I was telling the researcher that something similar had happened to me about two to three months after John's cousin had died in 1985.

I awoke one night to see Irene standing at the bottom of our bed. "Elsie," she said, "I've just come to tell you that I've met mother and dad – and Anne is there." She sounded so happy. "And all the dogs are there too," she added. "There's no need for you to worry at all." And then she was gone.

Anne was Irene's daughter who had died when she was five days old. She would have been in her forties had she lived and the dogs referred to were Scottish terriers. As long as I had known them there was always one there. Each had lived until it died of natural causes, then it was replaced by another and, if I remember correctly, they were all called Jock.

It reminded me that I had had a similar message for her when her father had died two years before this happened.

Jane was interested, "This often happens to people who have experienced contact with UFOs," she said. This was something which I had not associated with my sighting, but she had thoroughly researched each of the fifteen aspects on which the series of programmes was being made and had spoken to over a hundred people in doing so. Her knowledge regarding the paranormal was extensive.

In conversation the name 'Linda' had been mentioned. It is a common enough name but it seemed to ring a bell. Of course, I realised, there was a Linda on the 'Kilroy' programme. She had missed the train from Manchester on that day and had travelled to London by plane. It was she who was scheduled to speak before me on that programme – and neither of us was invited to say a word. We wondered if it would be the same Linda. How strange if it were.

I had arrived at the studios at 10.00 a.m. and had already seen the recording of the first programme. The people in that one left and lunch was to be served at 12.30. This gave me forty-five minutes to see the sights of Tottenham Court Road and find out where McDonald's was, as I was to meet Douglas there at 4.15 p.m. I'd had a headache most of the morning and felt the fresh air would help to relieve it. It was lovely weather and the sun had come out so it was very pleasant as I walked into the street. I found McDonald's and decided to walk down one side of Tottenham Court Road and back along the other. How I wished I hadn't. The pavements were crowded with people rushing in all directions and crossing the roads was a nightmare. They were full, really full, of stop and start vehicles and more contaminated air I have never breathed. It was full of fumes. "But this is London, mum," my son had said later. How I would appreciate the very fresh, if blustery air of Church Stowe when I returned that evening. We may not have shops, streetlights, pubs, a bus service or much traffic, but fresh air is really plentiful.

I returned to the studios finding that lunch was ready and that Timothy Good and Hilary Evans had arrived to take part in the programme. Tim, who is the author of *Above Top Secret* and *Alien Liaison*, has travelled the world interviewing hundreds of people who claim to have seen UFOs and aliens. He is convinced that they exist and is certain that mankind has already captured dead aliens and their spacecraft. Hilary has spent twenty years putting UFO sightings to the test and believes that, in principle, he can give a possible explanation for any case you can come up with. He had spoken on the subject of 'Balls of Light' at the ICUR conference, and with Jane we talked about the series which was to be shown on ITV from January to April 1990.

Linda's train was due to arrive at Euston at 12.30 p.m. but by 1.15 p.m. she had not arrived at the studio and it was nearly time for the briefing session before the recording. Tim and Hilary were concerned, but were assured by Jane that I was standing by to take her place if she did not arrive in time. Hilary had heard my story at the conference the previous July but Tim was not there. Jane gave him a copy of the account which she had in her file. He read it and was expressing his interest when Linda and her husband Trevor appeared.

What a surprise – there was immediate recognition. It was the same Linda I had met on the Kilroy programme and this time I would hear her story. Every one disappeared for briefing and later Trevor and I watched the programme being recorded. Linda's experience was really much more sensitive than mine had been.

The people taking part in the final programme of the series arrived. The subject was dreams and in that group was a lady whose dreams always came true. Before leaving the studio, Trevor and I were given a guided tour and visited the gallery where numerous people involved in highly technical operations ensured that the recording proceeded smoothly and that the series, when complete, would be highly successful.

How strange that Linda and I should have met again in this way. We had both been selected to take part in that recording by a complete stranger who had judged each of our experiences to be relevant for inclusion in that series on different aspects of the paranormal, so proving that there is no line that can, or should, be drawn between UFOs and other aspects of the subject. They are all part and parcel of the same thing.

On that day listening to people recounting their strange experiences gave credibility and relevance to some of the unusual things that were happening to me at that time.

The previous day had been my birthday and my present from John was to be a navy blue suit. Instead of the usual shopping spree to Milton Keynes or Northampton, I had felt that I was being guided towards Leamington Spa, a place we had only visited twice for shopping, the last time being about three years before.

It poured with rain as we set out and was still raining when we arrived. We decided that as we did not know the town at all well we would find a marker and work outwards from there, so we chose Goodness Foods, a health store, because there was also one at Weedon which I frequently used.

For nearly two hours we visited dress shops only to find everywhere we called, that in December 1989 the 'in' colours for Winter were red and black and on each occasion we were told that navy blue was a Spring colour, also that the Spring Collections would be on sale after the Christmas holidays. Another helpful thing we discovered was that at that time I appeared to be pear-shaped, needing a size sixteen jacket but a size eighteen skirt.

We had two hours of allocated parking time and it was almost up so we made out way along a different street towards where we had parked the car. There we saw another shop which looked promising. "Sorry Madam," was the reply after explaining what I was looking for, "we don't sell anything above a size sixteen." A very understanding lady must have noticed the disappointment. She suggested places to which we could go, but we had already visited them and were on our way back to the car.

"Oh, if you have a car," she added, "have you tried Warwick?" We had never been shopping in Warwick and in the pouring rain, home seemed to be the most comfortable place to be, but she said that there was a shop there which had a vast range of lady's clothing up to size twenty-two. She was sure that it would be worth a visit.

So, after explaining that we were to go past Warwick Castle to the

126

traffic lights and turn left into Jury Street, that this shop was just on the right as we entered and that, with a bit of luck, we might be able to park outside the shop, we decided to go.

It is difficult to know where Leamington Spa ends and Warwick begins. When passing through you could be forgiven if you thought that it was one continuous built up area. We found the Castle, turned at the traffic lights into Jury Street, went along it and turned round. We did eventually park outside the shop but part of the car was over the double yellow no-parking lines, so John said he would stay with the car whilst I went into the shop to see if there was anything I liked, so he stood in the rain looking out for a traffic warden. Unfortunately it was not to be my lucky day and we decided to go home.

On the way home we stopped for lunch at a lovely pub by the side of the Grand Union Canal then continued our journey. Arriving at home I picked up the morning mail which had been delivered during our absence. There were eight envelopes, most of which were Christmas cards and I stacked them neatly with the smallest and narrowest on the top, put them in the kitchen and took off my coat.

Then I looked at the mail. The one on top was an envelope with a window, obviously not a Christmas card. On closer inspection it had a stamped message on the top – "If undelivered please return to 20-22 Jury Street, Warwick." How strange! We had been sent to that very street, of which we had never heard until that morning – and now in the post was correspondence from another address in it.

John looked at it. "I bet that's from the Heart of England Building Society," he said. "I saw it this morning whilst I was waiting outside the dress shop. It was almost opposite where I stood." I opened the envelope – and it was.

We wondered what odds the bookies would have given for something like that happening?

A few days after this I was to find another coincidence connected with that visit.

Two days before our trip to Leamington Spa I had wanted a certain type of stuffing mix for my Christmas turkey. I had bought it previously from Goodness Foods' shop at Weedon. On that day there was none so the Manager had phoned around their other shops to see if he could get some for me and had found two packets which would be at Weedon for me to collect the following week.

Two days after my visit to Leamington Spa I called at the shop. There had been a misunderstanding and they were still at their original destination. Then I asked from where they were coming. "Our shop in Leamington Spa," he said. It was the very same one that we had singled out as a marker – and had we known we could have collected them ourselves.

What a week this was turning out to be, but more was yet to come.

* * *

Derrick Butcher is Kate's husband and his business involves the use of a computer. On hearing about this account I was writing about the years from 22nd November 1978, he very kindly volunteered to put it all on disc and became increasingly interested in everything I did.

As time went by he became more involved and as he also had an interest in photography he accompanied me along the route of my experience taking slides at strategic points which would enable me to illustrate the talks which I had been asked to give at Adult Education Centres.

I phoned Derrick to thank him for his slides and to tell him how well the talk at Knuston Hall had gone, also how I was able to use the A4 sized diagrams he had produced on his computer to make overhead projector transparancies.

"A very strange thing has happened to my computer," he said. He told me how he had received two discs in the post and that when he had used them in the computer it had gone haywire. He had since received a letter from the firm to say that there was a virus on the discs and giving instructions how to cure it. He had also taken advice from the makers of his own equipment. This had all helped for a time but after about three hours it started all over again – and he was in this predicament when I phoned.

Whilst I was talking he was trying to remedy the situation, but to no avail. I sensed his frustration.

"I will talk to my UFO friends," I said, "because if they intend my book to be completed and published the only way that will happen will be for your computer to work properly – as it is all in there." Then, I added, "if anyone could hear this conversation they'd think I was going mad!" We laughed and I rang off leaving him to try and sort out his problems whilst I continued to unpack my shopping, tittering away to myself at the thought of other people's comments had they been there to hear the conversation.

Almost immediately the phone rang. "You'll never guess what's happened," said Derrick's cheerful voice, "a menu came on to the screen which didn't appear to give me any choice, but I pressed a key – and now everything is all right. It's perfect."

About six weeks after this Derrick and Kate visited us. The computer was still functioning properly.

* * *

Douglas, Terri's father, was driving home through Oxfordshire listening to Radio 1 on his car radio. Suddenly a loud crackle distorted the sound so he flicked through the other channels.

"Is there anything that has happened locally that you can tell us about?" a voice asked.

"Well there's not one in Oxfordshire but there was one in Northamptonshire," was the reply. Having been born in that county and now living in Weedon, Douglas decided he'd listen.

"There was a teacher there who had an unusual encounter at Weedon in 1978," continued the voice.

"Not MUM!" said Douglas aloud – but it was.

There, at that moment, over the air, he found himself listening to an account of my UFO sighting being given by John Spencer.

* * *

A NUFORC meeting was also scheduled around this time and points raised during a talk at a previous one and information I had been given after it were still worrying me. It was essential that I should receive some advice to clarify the situation.

I knew who could assist me, as she would have the answers which would help me to come to terms with it, but she had moved away from the home I used to visit and I did not have her new address. It was not a matter of life or death, but to see her and to talk to her would certainly ease my mind.

The meeting was to be held on the Saturday afternoon and this was the Wednesday before. Joan had invited me to join her and Frank for coffee after my visit to the hairdresser and I was just telling them how I wished I could find this friend as I needed her help. At that point in the conversation a dark-haired lady passed by the window. As this was at the back of the house Frank went to see if he could help as she looked as if she were expecting to find something or somebody.

She was a stranger to Joan and we were even more surprised when Frank brought her into the house to see me. "This lady is looking for an address in Stowe," he said, "and as you live there I thought you would be able to help."

I was given the name of the house and the address and it did seem to ring a bell, but to be sure I asked if she could tell me the name of the people who lived there – and she named my elusive friend. She went on to say that she thought the village we were in was Stowe and having found the village hall and followed the instructions she had been given, she thought she was in the right house.

"How strange," said Joan, "we were just talking about her and wondering how to contact her, then you appeared." I directed the visitor to the address she required and she thanked us and left. Joan and I sat looking at each other in amazement. "Someone, somewhere certainly knew I needed that help," I said, "and has offered me a clue."

The following day I rang the owner of that address and found that he had offered my friend a room in his home to use for her spiritual group meetings and readings. He passed on my message and she contacted me later in the day. I was able to go and see her on the Friday, in time to enable me to come to terms with the information I had received and to help me to understand what was beginning to happen to me.

"The spirits work in strange ways," she told me.

"Well, I think my UFO friends had something to do with it, too," I said.

"Quite possibly," she replied.

Chapter Nineteen

THE KNOCK-ON EFFECT

Around this time I began to notice that my life had become full of interesting and very varied involvements, and the saying that: 'One thing always leads to another' seemed very appropriate.

I had been interviewed by a group of researchers, about my UFO experience, and since the ICUR Conference it was becoming generally known that I was willing to speak openly about it. I was absolutely certain by then that by doing so I would find all the answers I needed. So when I was asked to take part in a course that would include a section on UFOs of the Close Encounter kind, I readily agreed.

There were not many CE4 Witnesses, as we were then being called, who were speaking openly and it was something of a novelty for the public to come face-to-face with someone who had undergone such an experience. I now had my visual aids to illustrate my talks. I had used them at Knuston Hall and had enjoyed my day there, so this offer did not appear to be too daunting. Little did I know!

In order to advertise this course many people in all types of the media had been notified, so I was interviewed by a freelance journalist and one from *Syndicated Features*. Then I found that a tabloid newspaper had also received information about it and one of their reporters rang to see if he could interview me too. New experiences for me, all of them, and I was soon to learn something about the power of the press.

The article in the tabloid, when it was printed, was headed 'HUNTED BY A UFO' in letters nearly two inches high. To say that it was sensational was, in my opinion, an understatement and it caused a flurry of excitement in many quarters which five days later had caused me to be exhausted enough to sleep the clock round.

"Victims warn of a mind-blowing threat to Earth," it announced and said that the speakers, of whom I was to be one, were "all set to shock Britain's UFO-watchers, for their true-life close encounters have convinced them that aliens are not only watching us but hunting us."

My interview with the reporter had been taped so that the details of my experience were accurate enough, but what he failed to do was to explain to the readers that these sensational statements were his own interpretation of the information he had collected during his interviews and not the facts that had been stated. I was by then very used to seeing these kinds of headlines and insinuations, but I did think this one went a bit 'over-the-top'. However, it was the word 'hunted' which caused me to put myself into the reporter's shoes and try to understand why he had used that particular word and when I did reach a conclusion I had to admit that it was a logical word to use. After all, from the time of the first tightening sensation about 1.30 p.m. to the final one after 7.00 p.m. was around six hours and I was by then becoming convinced that during all that time I was under the surveillance of the occupants of that UFO. A long time to be watched and followed – and controlled. If the object had been an animal, the description of 'hunting' would have been very apt.

The reaction caused by this article was in some ways similar to that which I received following that first report, headed 'UFO Stops Car', which was written by Peter Aengenheister for the *Chronicle & Echo* newspaper in 1978. The phone seemed to ring continuously with people wanting to share their own experiences or to hear more about mine and one of the first was from a researcher for the BBC1 TV programme, Daytime Live. It came as a complete surprise and gave me a most entertaining twenty-four hours.

The programme researcher had read the newspaper article and wanted to know more about it. "We would love to cover it on a programme," she said, so it was arranged that I would take part in a programme a few days later.

I spent the night before the recording in a hotel so that I could be at the TV studio in time for rehearsals when, much to my surprise, I found I was to be involved in the introduction to the programme also.

"What do you think about UFOs?" Judy Spiers asked the viewers. "Well, Elsie Oakensen's convinced that she's been spied on by aliens." "Why?" she asked me.

"Because on my way home in 1978 I encountered so many strange things that just could not have been man-made," I answered.

This was a new experience for me as in four of the previous television

132

programmes in which I had taken part it was Jenny's book which was being promoted and I was only there to tell my story as a support for that promotion.

This time I was appearing in my own right and thanks to Jenny I was now confident enough to cope with any type of question which came my way.

After our six-minute interview, Judy Spiers handed the programme over to the presenter of the next item. I was released from my microphone, left the set and was guided back to the hospitality room. There I was to meet others who were taking part in that day's programme which was being shown on the monitor when we arrived. As I entered the room I was confronted by a man who said he was an alien (not an unusual occurrence in a television studio, it had happened to me before) and he proceeded to give me a lecture on Einstein's Theory of Relativity – I think!

Thankfully someone else then took his attention and I was joined by another young lady. She said that she had enjoyed the programme and would I be willing to record an interview for a show on BBC Midland Radio. This I did and listeners in seven Midland counties were later able to listen to the whole account of my UFO experience.

On my return home I received a call from *Take a Break* magazine. A young lady wanted to know if the story in the newspaper was *really* true.

Then a lady who rings for a chat after every television appearance I make said she had a photograph of a UFO similar in shape to the one I had seen (an artist's impression had been on the screen during the interview). She had put the photograph in the post for me to see and it arrived the following day. It was indeed similar, but as it was 'for my eyes only' I felt duty bound to return it immediately.

The next call was from Radio Belfast asking if I would describe my sighting in more detail for their listeners. This I did on the phone from home, sitting in the kitchen and hoping that no-one would ring the front door bell during that time. It is rather a loud one, and fortunately no-one did.

Local newspapers are always interested when someone in their area warrants a mention in a national newspaper and the *Northampton Citizen* was no different. An interview was arranged for the next day and a photographer was to accompany the reporter, but I assume that something much more newsworthy must have happened on that day as, although I was at home, no-one arrived.

The course went really well. The morning's programme included a variety of videos including one of the hypnosis of a close encounter witness and one of a TV interview with the author of a book which contained information about his own encounters with alien entities. There was also a series of slides about a local sighting.

Immediately after lunch I did my talk but unfortunately could not use the slides. On that day the sunshine was so bright that the curtains in the building proved to be inadequate to darken the room at that time, and the best effect could not be gained from the slides, so I managed without them.

A few days later I received a call from the Wogan show. A programme on UFOs was being planned for sometime in the future. This also resulted from the article in the newspaper. I was the first person contacted by the researcher and told my story again over the telephone. Perhaps later I shall be contacted again but there is no guarantee. As with Thames Television Stories in the Night they will obviously have to talk to others and hear their stories so that they can select the right people for a successful show. I had a similar call from a researcher from Them & Us, a new BBC TV programme due to start in the summer, but obviously my story was not of the type which they wanted to cover and I heard no more about it.

Then there was one from Peter Wynn, a researcher for Channel 4's Clive Anderson Talks Back show. It appeared that there I qualified as a person with an unusual story to tell. I had a visit from Peter who checked that my story was not a hoax and I was asked to appear in a later series.

It was about this time that I decided to try and discover what had happened as a follow up to the other interviews which I had given to newspaper reporters, as it seems so often that after the interview has taken place they do whatever they decide with the report and very few have let me know when and where it would be published. I found that one had been accepted by an editor of a newspaper and that he had 'sat on it', so it was now too late to use it. Another was accepted by a magazine but was not published when it came to the notice of the Editor that facts describing the experiences of the abductees mentioned in it had not been finally checked with us before being passed on to her.

Numerous people that I met socially commented on the Daytime Live programme or the newspaper article, but one stands out as being more unusual than the rest. A lady from Nether Heyford whom I saw at a dance in Daventry told me she had received through the post the cutting from the newspaper. It was from a relative who lived in Rye. She had sent it partly because the map printed in it showed Nether Heyford, but really because that lady had lived in Church Stowe herself in her younger days and of course knew the area well.

Then Reg Pinckheard came into the picture again. As Vice-chairman of NUFORC he was always on the look out for UFOs and anybody who had seen one. In conversation he had heard about a sighting in the area. He produced the necessary sighting forms to collect the details and volunteered to help the witness fill them in. "Thank you," the family had said politely, "but we'd rather see that lady who was on television." Reg was not in the least bit put out. He rang to tell me and was very amused by it all.

I went along and the problem seemed to be that only part of my story had been told on the programme and the family wanted to hear the rest of it as well. During the hour and a half I was there both the forms and the story were completed.

Another phone call I received at this time was interesting too. It was from a man who lives locally. He said that he had been visiting his parents in the North of England and they had saved the article from the newspaper for him. He wanted me to know that he had been driving his car between Nether Heyford and Weedon when the lights had gone out and the radio had stopped. The following week the same thing happened at exactly the same spot. His car was checked each time but nothing was found to be faulty. The reason for his call was to tell me that he was as sure as he could be that on one of these occasions it coincided with my sighting.

I also learned of a car stop and possible loss of time on Oak Tree Hill (just outside Church Stowe) at the same time as my sighting. This, I was told, was a claim made by another local man to a group of people in a public house that very same evening. Unfortunately he has never wished to be interviewed.

* * *

By the time 1990 had arrived I had come to terms with the excitement of it all, the ridicule, the understanding, the feeling that there was a purpose to it – and it seemed as if I was being guided along. My confidence in myself and my ability to do things had returned. I had become a positive-thinking person again who knew that nothing was impossible if I set my mind to do it.

The series of events described in this chapter all took place during a period of seven weeks. They show how at certain times one contact can snowball into a number of involvements – all of which my new positive-thinking personality enjoyed to the full whilst it lasted, but at the end of that time I was both emotionally and physically exhausted and the most urgent need then was for me to recharge my batteries.

This was quite easy to do as I always felt that in this I had some external help. I would find that no matter how necessary I thought it to be to continue with this writing, absolutely nothing would come into my mind. But later, when refreshed, information flowed freely and I was able to record it all again.

Often people to whom I have spoken have remarked too that relative occurrences and coincidences have come is spasms, alternating a period of excitement and fatigue with one of relative peace.

Chapter Twenty

ANSWERS?

Through a phone call I received from Wales in June 1989, I was made aware that a large number of people world-wide were expecting a catastrophe of much larger proportions than I could possibly have imagined and that it was much closer than I could have expected.

When I had read *Abduction*, the date 1992 seemed to jump out at me each time it was written, but here was a voice asking, "You know about the holocaust, don't you?" and going on to explain that a natural catastrophe was expected in that same year with freak conditions causing earthquakes, volcanic eruptions and flooding and that landmasses would disappear causing the present world's maps to become unrecognisable.

As I understood the message in that phone call, these predictions which had come through mediums world-wide, all linked with information given by UFO contactees who were described as 'Ambassadors for a higher intelligence'.

The speaker's opinion was that Jenny's book could have been a vehicle to bring awareness to people, to make them think and maybe to encourage them to form a nucleus of groups working towards lessening the impact in the future, as at that time, he said, there was a very strong feeling to gather people together in order to deal practically with future events.

During his call he also listed the names of people whom he felt I should contact, as he had heard that I now felt compelled to examine the details of my close encounter and record the changing effects it was having on my life, especially since its inclusion in that very same book – and he felt that these people could all contribute something in helping me to find answers to my questions.

By this time I had known Graham for four months. He had felt drawn

137

towards Northampton and had joined our UFO group. He was also contacting certain people throughout the country as this was what he felt was the right thing for him to do.

I noted the names supplied; they were people from all parts of the country and, as high telephone bills are not very popular in our household, I decided to keep them for future reference. I felt that if I really were to play an important part in some future group then someone else would make the effort to contact me as Graham had done.

I did not have long to wait. The next day one of the people on that list phoned, chatted and added more names to it – and the following day another one spoke to me. Then, on the day after that, Graham rang also and in those following seventy-two hours I had learned that answers and understanding would be coming in steps; that the information would not only be fascinating but would also be confusing; that there would not only be a physical change on our planet, but a spiritual change in our way of thinking; that up to 1992 there would be a build-up of UFO activity and that there would be a parting of the ways of those who did believe and those who didn't.

Again the phrase 'Ambassadors for a higher intelligence' was quoted and over those four days it was made abundantly clear to me that because of my UFO encounter I would definitely be playing a part in all this. I had never really thought of myself as an ambassador for anything. This was a very daunting thought. If this were really to be so, I only hoped that I could live up to all the expectations that would be made of me.

*   *   *

One of the people named on my list was a man I came to know as Gary H. He phoned me and claimed, as Graham had done, to have answers to all my questions and we also found that we had several things in common. He had, like me, had an abduction experience which had also featured in a book written by Jenny Randles. He lived in my part of the country and, unbeknown to me at that time, was also a member of NUFORC though I had not met him at a meeting.

He talked of happenings in the Bible which he related to UFOs and preferred to refer to aliens as 'Angels'. He told me a little about his own experience and suggested books I should read. He also gave me one reason why I was 'picked' (his word) by a UFO. He said that everything would be coming to a head soon and that I would be involved purely and simply because I was "not ordinary and not exceptional".

He had heard about Graham and wanted to meet us both. He said he would speak to Ernest Still to see if the three of us could meet together after the next NUFORC meeting in September.

At that meeting he was the speaker and started a talk which was to take two meetings to complete. He spoke about the Bible and UFO involvement with the stories therein. Things that had to me always seemed unbelievable had, to him, a logical explanation and were illustrated with up to date terminology.

It was fascinating to listen to him and it reminded me of our middle son, David, when he was young. He could always find a scientific explanation for anything unusual which happened in the Bible.

Some people at that meeting recorded the talk. I wish I had been able to do so too, then I would have been able to refer to the accounts accurately here, but I had no tape recorder with me and I cannot remember it all in detail, but everything made sense and I could understand it. I had never before heard anyone with such a full and detailed knowledge of the Bible. Every point raised and every question asked of him was answered with a very comprehensive reply. Nothing worried him. His manner was calm and confident and he spoke with such authority that it would have been difficult not to believe him.

I'd had one flash-back during this talk to when David was about ten or eleven years old and now I had another to the time when I was an even younger child.

My mother belonged to the Church of England faith and my brother Ted and I regularly attended Sunday School at St. Nicholas' Church at Potterspury when we were small, but after a time we were taken away and sent to Sunday School in the Congregational Church, also in the same village. I cannot remember exactly how old I was but I did ask "Why?" and was given to understand that at church we had been taught by older children, whereas at chapel we would be taught by adults.

So, each Sunday, both morning and afternoon we walked, often reluctantly, to the other end of the village to join in the services. My father came from a family of Congregationalists and his mother and her sister, who lived near to us were also members of the congregation – a point which we were to find was not always to our advantage! But there is one important thing I do remember about Sunday School at the chapel.

It was there that I was introduced to the knowledge that Christ would one day return to the earth. The question of when was put by enquiring young minds and the year 2000 was quoted. There, in the 1930s, we could not imagine that date nearly seventy years into the future, but I can remember working out that on that date I would be seventy-two years old, if I lived until then. No-one, however, could explain exactly how Christ would return to the earth, or where, but as young as I was I felt a tremendous compulsion to live long enough to witness the scene.

At the previous NUFORC meeting, in order to help me understand what was beginning to happen to me, Graham had written a dossier listing the information which had come to him since his abduction mainly through dreams. It was nine pages long and as, at that time, I was in my infancy regarding what I now know to be the experience of psychic phenomena, he handed it to me, but asked me not to read page nine as he considered that I was not yet in a position to understand and cope with all the implications of what he had been told to expect as the final outcome of it all.

What I read on those eight pages I could relate to and it was during this time that I realised that Graham had already experienced some of the strange things which had been happening to me and we were able to discuss them more fully. I was also able to see at last that I really was not alone. Gradually I was meeting more people who had also been abducted and the whole situation was becoming more interesting and very intriguing.

After the meeting was over and we had vacated the room we continued to talk in groups outside, then Gary H. invited Graham and his mother and me to sit in his car, as he said there was something he felt it was time that we should know.

Hurriedly Graham passed to me the sheaf of papers he had brought to the previous meeting and said that he thought I should now read page nine. This I did and it mentioned the preparation for the coming of Christ. I handed back the papers not really taking it in. Everything suddenly seemed to be in a rush.

Gary H. joined us. He wrote some words on to a sheet of paper and talked about Nostradamus and his prophesies. It was a continuation of his talk and I was thinking again of how interested David would have been if he'd been there. He then spoke about anagrams and about how a letter was always changed in them according to Nostradamus's rules.

Then he proceeded to adjust the letters to form a statement, explaining why as he did so.

Then he looked at us and asked, "Do you understand what I am saying?"

Graham and Valerie said they did. This was the news they had been expecting for some time.

My mind was in a turmoil, so much had happened that afternoon that seemed almost incredible. He handed me the paper and I read aloud the resulting statements from the two anagrams. I looked at him. His gaze was steady.

They described a role in which he was to play a prominent part "And are you implying that I am going to be part of all of this too?" I asked.

"Yes," he replied.

"*Why me?*" was my immediate response.

"Because of your love and compassion," he answered, "and because you have worked with children. You won't be misquoted or led into saying something that you don't want to. Also, you are a 'green' person."

I felt absolutely shattered and was sure that my head would burst. I was just beginning to accept that it was normal under the circumstances to hear strange noises in my ear and Graham was guiding me through each stage so that there was a gentle build-up of understanding towards the final revelation of events that were to come. But here it was – now.

I felt as if I had been catapulted into space. It was the last thing I had expected and I was quite unprepared to hear it. How on earth was I going to cope with something like that? It was certainly not something you could bring out in an ordinary conversation over the garden fence – and, in any case, Gary H. had not gone public!

I felt it best to tell no-one at all until I had come to terms with it in my own way. I wondered how long it would take, but at least I was not alone. Graham and Valerie had been entrusted with the information too and that became a great comfort in the weeks which followed.

* * *

My first meeting with Gary H. had been a surprise to say the least. When I left him on that Saturday I really was in a state of shock, not knowing what to think and not daring to tell anyone, mainly because it was something which only he could tell the public, but also because I would not have known how to cope with the questions which would have been directed at me after doing so.

It was on that day that I realised how little I knew about the UFO phenomenon and many other now obviously related subjects. At that time I had met only Graham and now Gary H. who had had abduction experiences and who had talked to me about them in very great detail, so I was not aware of all the information coming through those who claim to have contact with alien entities, or in fact claim to be alien spirits reincarnated into human bodies. As time went on I was to meet such people. How brave to admit something like that to people who do not understand it or how it could possibly be.

At one meeting I had heard a man say that he had interviewed a disciple at the crucifixion of Christ. That was way beyond my comprehension but the person concerned was very convincing. Later it was explained to me that this could have been possible through astral travel, or that perhaps this man had been a medium with a guide who was extremely old and it was he who may have been there at that time. That information could have come through him.

As I got to know him better I was astounded to find that Gary H. possessed an intimate knowledge of a vast range of subjects. No matter how trivial a point seemed to be he would always find a solution. Nothing was too much trouble for him.

One afternoon when he called at our home to bring some information which he considered to be appropriate for me to read, I was to find myself grateful for his help. He had heard that one of my interests was craftwork and that I was in the process of making a patchwork jacket. He asked to see it and was impressed that it already contained 485 pieces of material all stitched together by hand. It was almost at the stage where I would have to decide on the fastenings. Here I had a problem. There were many on sale which I could use but I felt it needed something which was, like the jacket, created by hand.

I needed to look no further. Gary H. had a suggestion – knots and loops – and at the next NUFORC meeting he presented me with examples of some he thought would be appropriate. I selected those which I decided would be most suitable. He supplied the instructions and I made them. My problem was solved.

That jacket was to receive mention at a future gathering when he remarked that the pattern on it was made in a variety of different sizes of triangle, something which I had not intentionally set out to do.

The triangle is an important shape in both spiritualism and ufology I was later to be told and it was with interest that I joined a group led by Gary H. on a visit to an area which included what must be one of the strangest buildings ever built. Gary describes himself as having a fascination for triangles so it was no wonder that our afternoon out included Triangular Lodge at Rushton in Northamptonshire.

This is a very beautiful but most unusual 16th century building, the architecture of which is cleverly used to express the personal philosophy and religious beliefs of its Roman Catholic builder, Sir Thomas Tresham.

As it symbolises the Trinity, everything is built in threes. It has three sides, three floors, trefoil-shaped windows and triangular gables on each side. Sometimes known as the Warrener's Lodge, it was built during the years 1593-95 and is considered to be one of the strangest small buildings ever devised.

I shall not go into the reason for that visit for that is Gary's story. I shall just record that we had a most interesting afternoon, which also included other historical buildings in the area and was on, what turned out to be one of those glorious days in the very long, hot summer of 1990.

Chapter Twenty-one

WITNESS-DRIVEN INVESTIGATION

By February 1990 it had become obvious that the ICUR Conference had indeed been a stepping-stone to further involvement in the UFO phenomenon. My understanding about karma and aura grew as I came into contact with many new people. I had had an experience of on-site visualisation and was by then considered to be contaminated with regard to hypnosis because of my ever-growing interest in the subject.

Witness-driven investigation, however, was something of which I had no knowledge at all and it was with surprise and great enthusiasm that I agreed to join a group of close encounter witnesses at a meeting organised by Ken Phillips, in order to put this theory to the test.

To do this I had one more hurdle to cross myself that would finally convince me that I could now feel fully confident in carrying out everything which, before my enforced retirement, I would have done without giving it a second thought. This invitation offered that opportunity as, in order to attend that meeting, I had to travel alone to London. It also offered the kind of experience for which I had been waiting for eleven and a half years, and wild horses would not have kept me away.

I had been furnished with the details of travel and this involved going by British Rail to Euston, then a trip on the underground followed by a bus ride. This, I thought, was all too adventurous for me and instead I decided to go by taxi from Euston to the venue of the meeting. It seemed simpler that way. However, a week before the event, because I had two journeys forthcoming which would necessitate rail travel, I had invested in a Senior Citizen Railcard.

The first surprise on the day of the meeting was when John left me at Milton Keynes station saying that, as I now had a railcard, the fare would be much cheaper so there would be no need for him to use his Barclaycard for it and I was left to purchase the ticket myself.

The second was when I was asked if my journey would include the underground? "Yes," I replied. "And London Transport?" Yes, again. I found myself with a One-day Travelcard, the cost of which included all these forms of transport. The charge for this comprehensive fare was £4.75 which came as quite a shock as my previous train journey to London, albeit from Northampton station, had cost £19.80. I had always envied those passengers who could walk past the ticket collectors and just show a ticket. It was a much quicker system and on that day I was able to do just that.

On arrival at Euston Station I weighed up the pros and cons of paying for a taxi and opted to use my ticket. I found that it was designed to be used in the machines on the underground and I negotiated that part of the journey with ease, although it was the first time I had ever done so alone.

Arriving in daylight once more, using the street map supplied, I easily found the bus stop and with the help of a friendly young passenger found a bus going in the right direction, although it was a different number from the one which had been suggested. The result was that I had to alight before the anticipated stop and finish with a twenty-minute walk to the meeting place. The weather was windy but fine and I arrived safely at my destination – having passed another hurdle in my quest to regain my confidence in travelling alone in unfamiliar parts of the country.

* * *

This meeting was the first of its kind to be held in the United Kingdom and was called with the specific aim of bringing together a group of people with varying experiences of UFO encounters. There were fourteen other people present and they came from all parts of England and Scotland.

To my delight, after twelve years, I was at last able to talk through my experiences with others classed as being in the same category. Proof indeed that I was not alone.

It was an afternoon worth waiting for and the feeling of excitement that I had whilst journeying there changed to amazement as I listened to each one explaining what had happened to them. There was such a variety of experiences being described that I could fully understand the looks of disbelief I had encountered over the years when I had been asked to speak about mine.

It had been agreed before the meeting began that everything should be recorded, but that it would all remain confidential to those present on that day. We were each promised a copy of the video and one would be sent to Budd Hopkins who works with a similar group in New York.

Most of those present had not spoken publicly about their experiences before and some were so nervous that they had to be calmed by a member of the group. That impressed me greatly at the time and I wondered why it should.

The UFO experience seemed to have had a profound effect on everyone present. Since their encounters some had found they had developed new skills. Most had become more psychically aware, one had become more technically minded. Others mentioned clairvoyant visions, one was able to do automatic writing, another now had an artistic ability. Writing poetry, composing songs and writing scripts for videos and films were all accomplishments attributed to the UFO experience. An interest in the Bible was very prominent and a caring attitude towards people and animals had also manifested itself. One witness who admitted to being illiterate before his experience can now read and write and spell. I wondered if my life would go along the same lines as any of the others. Within weeks I was to find that I had an answer to that question.

The first two meetings were held at the home of Janice Georgiou, also a Close-Encounter Witness, but later BUFORA provided a meeting place at the London Business School and we met regularly at two-monthly intervals. At these, topics and discussions were prompted by the witnesses themselves, going off in any direction which any of us felt understanding was required. We talked through our experiences and counselled each other. New witnesses were invited to join us and the 'old-stagers' were able to assure them that immediately following their experiences they need not, through uncertainty, go through such a traumatic period as we had done.

The meetings were witness-driven and gradually we found that, from each other, we were able to receive information to which we could relate. We had at first felt alone. Now we no longer did. An understanding of

146

what had happened, and why it had happened, in time became acceptable to us all.

* * *

Points raised were sometimes illustrated by videos and more discussion was then generated. One which particularly interested me at one meeting referred to corn circles.

A television programme on the subject had been videoed showing the reporters describing a huge circle in the corn and sounds that were being picked up from certain areas within it. At the end of the programme one member of our group who was known to have flashes of recognition and can accurately describe people he has never met, reported that he had just for a second seen a UFO hovering above the field with a transparent barrier-like thing (the shape of a pastry-cutter) below it. This was lowered into the corn and power from below the UFO swirled around within it before the UFO disappeared – leaving a circular shape of compressed corn below where it had been.

I somehow felt that I could relate to that suggestion. How else could I have sat in complete darkness on a fine, bright November day if there had not been a barrier of some kind surrounding the area in which I sat and excluding all the light from it? Could there be some connection between the two cases, I wondered? That is, of course, if a UFO was really responsible for that corn circle. If so, I suppose I was lucky not to have been flattened like the corn!

* * *

Dr. Alex Keul from Salzburg University in Austria was also present at one meeting. It was he who would be collating all the information gathered from the close encounter witnesses in the Anamnesis Tests which had been conducted by Ken Phillips at the ICUR Conference the previous July, also from witnesses elsewhere over a ten-year time-span. With him I had been able to raise the question of religious content in that questionnaire. Having described my encounter and answered over sixty questions about my life to that date it was no wonder that I could not remember all the topics which the questions covered.

The week before I had attended a NUFORC meeting where we had a talk about astrology.

The characteristics of people born under each of the star signs were being explained and the importance of the position of the moon, the sign of the fishes, was one point being emphasised. Not long before I had received my birth chart and a character analysis describing the celestial influences operating at the time of my birth and I had taken it with me to that meeting. Gary H. was sitting next to me and was interested. I passed it to him opened at the page headed 'Moon in Pisces'. In the tea interval he read:

"You are kind and sympathetic because of your sensitivity to the feelings of others. As you can be easily hurt inwardly you may develop a complex about others who try to hurt you." His next sentence was most unexpected.

"Most people who are 'picked on' by UFOs are very sensitive and very loving types of persons within," he said. "They can have a very crusty exterior, but this, in my opinion, is one of the reasons why you were picked."

He then read, " . . . given deep emotional attachment to religious, social and ethical values instilled in early childhood" and commented, "you have got a strong moral viewpoint. You may not consider yourself to be very religious, none the less religiousness in a person comes from the heart. It can't be given. It has to be there in the first instance and if there is a seed and it starts to grow then it will blossom. If it does blossom then that is what a Godly person is. Now, regardless of what others say, if they check into all UFO contacts or contactees they will find there is a strong 'religious' person. It doesn't matter whether they are Protestant, Catholic, Muslim or anything else before the event, and it can certainly be strengthened after, but if it is not there to begin with there is no way it will be there afterwards, except at a small level. Religion as to how you understand it in churches is not religious. It is something born in you. It is already there. If it is not in a person it is very difficult to put it there. Although you may not consider yourself to be religious, it was there, otherwise a UFO would not have contacted you."

I pointed out that for some years where religion had been concerned I had felt that I was in a wilderness not knowing which was the right one for me.

"That is totally irrelevant," I was told. "There are many good people who are termed 'Christians', who don't go to church. The Samaritan was the one who helped the person who had been robbed. He helped this

148

person – and all the people who should have helped him, all the 'religious' ones, didn't – and this is what Jesus was trying to get across. It is not going to church, external and all that. God dwells within a man or woman. You can't put it there just by going to church, by wearing a label and saying you are it, because that is not the way it works. The way a UFO contact takes place – it's that deep spirit within you that is being contacted, not the carcass – the spirit. It is the spirit that is being contacted."

I mentioned the Anamnesis Tests which were taking place in the hope that a common thread would be found to link all those who had experienced UFO contact and pointed out that if what he said were so, then it would not come through in those tests – and he agreed.

I informed Dr. Keul of this conversation as I wanted to know whether my assumption had been correct and welcomed this opportunity to ask him whether there was a possibility that this might come through in his research into trying to find that common thread in all those close encounter witnesses. He assured me that there were a number of questions on the religious aspects of our lives in his questionnaire – and dictated these to me.

- Do you belong to a church or religious group?
- Do you attend church or group meetings regularly?
- Is this religious belief due to mere convention or inner conviction?
- Do you consider the spiritual side of life to be important?

Dr. Keul and I then discussed the answers which I said I would have given to those questions and I became certain that they would separate the meanings of the two religious aspects as had been described. Also I was delighted that I had been proved wrong in thinking that the Anamnesis Tests may have missed that point.

He said he had received results from his tests and was hoping to begin to look for conclusive evidence later in the year. It was also interesting to know that he, like all UK investigators, was involved in his research purely because of a genuine interest in the subject. At the ICUR congress that test had seemed very important but Dr. Keul and Austria had seemed so far away. Now, having met him, I realised how much in common witnesses, investigators and researchers had, and how bound together they all were with this one common aim – to discover as much as they possibly could about all aspects of the UFO subject.

* * *

Because of my involvement with the group I, like the others, was asked to participate in a series of exercises which had been devised by members of the Society for Psychical Research in order to assess a range of psychic abilities. There were eight experiments, each with instructions and space on a separate sheet where impressions or information on the targets could be recorded and these exercises took place over seven consecutive days.

I attempted all the tests and returned my answers as requested at the end of the week, not feeling at all confident that I was then in any way endowed with psychic powers. Some months later the results were sent to Ken. They were not encouraging and confirmed my feelings at that time that I was not endowed with any psychic ability.

* * *

Soon after my contact with Graham he asked me if I had read a book entitled *Communion*. It was written by Whitley Strieber, an American author, and was an account of his contact with aliens. For exactly the same reason that I had read *Abduction*, I decided to read *Communion* – to see if there was anything in it to which I could relate and to see if his encounter was in any way similar to mine. I could find very little in common with him.

In August 1990 a film had been made of the story and members of BUFORA and our group were invited to a preview of its showing in London. I was there and watched it carefully, still hoping that perhaps I had missed some small point when I had read the book, but there was nothing until right at the end.

There, Ann Strieber, Whitley's wife, told him that he had changed since that Christmas night which had started the experience and that he had been given a wonderful gift.

I sat up in my seat. Not very many weeks before John had remarked that I "was becoming interested in some very strange things just lately." Then when she remarked about the 'wonderful gift' my mind was even more alert – at least I thought it was! Perhaps my hearing failed at that point but I cannot recall her saying what it was and it was something which I really needed to know.

The film was due to be released in this country on October 12th and much interest was aroused not only in the film but in my experience also. Newspapers, freelance journalists and TV companies when reviewing the film all needed examples of English sightings to illustrate their articles or programmes and thanks to the expertise of the Press Officer for BUFORA I became very heavily involved again. Another type of television interview took place. This time the crew and an interviewer came to our home, set up the cameras and lights in the front room and we chatted for twenty minutes.

When I had received the original phone call asking me to do this interview for BSB Television, I was also asked what I thought of the film. "Horrific," was my answer. Whilst the film had portrayed what Whitley Strieber had experienced I was really glad that I had only been fascinated by mine. I am sure that if I had encountered creatures such as were in that film I would not have dared to say a word about it to anyone. I felt it was extremely brave of him to publicise it in that way.

* * *

'Ken's meetings', as we called them then, continued at two-monthly intervals and were later held on the same day as the BUFORA Council meetings and the monthly lectures. In June 1990 when Ken gave an update of the Anamnesis programme at one of these, I stayed on and about ten of us related our experiences to a much wider audience.

We had become a very close group, all with an abduction experience in common, though all very different. As news of the group became better known, more witnesses felt able to join it and share their own experiences, gaining comfort from knowing that some of us had lived with ours for very much longer than they had.

It was also interesting to have feedback from the Anamnesis Tests and to hear that Dr. Keul had found some points which excited him enough to ask some of us to fill in an additional questionnaire. Graham and I were both in that group. Unfortunately, however, since that time, due to the closure of the Department of Parapsychology at Freilburg University, the Anamnesis Data evaluation has been suspended and no replacement faculty has yet been found to continue the project work.

At the end of the year I thought back to that first witness-driven investigation meeting where I had met other close encounter witnesses and where, after a search of over eleven years, I was to realise for the first time that about the only things we all had in common were a 'time loss' and ESP.

We were all different kinds of people living in different parts of the United Kingdom, each having seen a different model of UFO. Information retrieved under hypnosis was very varied and assorted types of alien were encountered.

Our reactions to these experiences ran through the whole range from fear to fascination. No two experiences were identical. No wonder UFO investigators and researchers are confused. No wonder the media and the public have difficulty in trying to the understand the phenomenon. At present there are so many variables, but I am sure that as time passes the confusion will be clarified and the reasons for it will become clearer.

Meetings of the group, now officially called the Witness Support Group, continue bi-monthly with differing aspects of CE4 abductions being discussed and counselling given to new abductees.

Slowly we come to terms with events. Most of us are speaking openly and we each try to come to terms with the expectation that we have a part to play in the future of our civilisation, though none of us is sure exactly what that will be. Some know more than others and feel they have started towards their goal. The rest of us can only wonder whether if, when the times comes, we will fit the requirements of that destiny.

Chapter Twenty-two

PSYCHIC PHENOMENA

At about the time when I became involved with Jenny and her book I began to suffer with a new kind of headache. I was used to headaches. I had learned to live with migraine from the age of twelve and at one period in my life I had gone through a time when I had only a few days free from it each month – but when you finally accept that pain is inevitable it becomes bearable and as I got older I treated it as just an inconvenience. I had a variety of tablets from a number of different doctors, got to know the different stages of it and how to cope.

Those headaches of course were on one side of my head and I'd had those which moved about quite a lot – but these new ones were completely different. They seemed to be centred between the eyes. "Sinusitis," my friends said, but tablets for that did not help. I could not understand what caused these, nor the intense pain, and after experimenting with a variety of tablets, including those I still had left over after a course of acupuncture had cured the migraine, I reluctantly visited the doctor. An infected nose was diagnosed and ointment prescribed.

Each time I had one of those headaches I applied the ointment until I realised that this was becoming a regular event and that they were always the same. Then I began to think that it could be a symptom of something much worse, so I paid another visit to the surgery and this time saw a different doctor.

"How can I help you?" I was asked.

"It's my nose," I answered feebly, and after a full examination came the judgement.

"It looks all right to me." It was a relief to hear this but it was hardly what I expected. However, I left feeling happier because it obviously was not serious and I was by then becoming aware of the fact that they never lasted very long. The pattern continued and I gradually came to terms with them also and was able to work out when to expect the next one.

On the Wednesday morning before the July 1989 NUFORC meeting another headache started. By Thursday morning it had taken hold and I felt really ill, but Friday was a new day and to my delight it was as if I had a new head. I felt wonderful.

These meetings were also held at two-monthly intervals. They were all so special to me as everyone present was on the same wavelength, but this one was to be different in two ways. Firstly I was looking forward to a talk on the subject of meditation by a number of the Theosophical Society and secondly because Graham was bringing Valerie, his mother, with him. She had supported Graham through the years following his abduction and I was very much looking forward meeting her.

Suddenly I remembered that three days before a previous meeting I had had one of those headaches and that it had lasted for forty-eight hours and I knew that the same thing would happen before this meeting and I knew also that this time I would notice exactly how it behaved.

As expected on the Wednesday evening it started with a dull ache at the top of my nose. This time I was not going to use the ointment nor take any tablets. On Thursday the pain was intense and I felt really ill, forcing myself to do only the things which were absolutely necessary. Had I put a 10p piece between my eyes, I would have noticed that all the pain would have been centred under it. On Thursday evening I went to bed early and on Friday woke up as lively as a cricket and all the pain had gone, just as I expected.

At the meeting on Saturday I mentioned my headaches independently to Valerie and to the speaker.

"Oh, that's your third eye," was the immediate response from both of them, "it is awakening."

"What's a third eye?" I asked. I had never heard of one.

It was explained to me as the awakening of psychic awareness. I did know that after abductions some witnesses do find themselves to have psychic powers. I had never felt that this has happened to me, but perhaps I did not interpret it in the right way. I knew that headache would happen and for some reason knew also that it was important that I should have the exact details to be able to describe it at a time when there were people around who would know exactly what it was.

* * *

The night time, even in our quiet village, is full of sounds but when I found a buzzing noise in my ears as I tried to sleep I was sure that tinnitus was the cause, but it was not continuous as I had always assumed it would be.

It had been happening most nights for some months and I began to accept it as part of the process of ageing. Then one night I felt, as with the headaches, that I should analyse it. It lasted only a minute or two and was not regular. It sounded like rushing water but was not very loud. I mentioned it to Graham when I next wrote to him and he knew exactly what I was talking about. He said it would come and go, so I entered it in my diary and waited to see if there was a pattern to it.

One night the sound changed to a droning noise in my left ear and to a lesser degree in my right one. It was like an aeroplane in the sky but was a louder, more concentrated sound. On that night I was able to check with John. He lifted his head off the pillow and listened. He could hear nothing. The sound was only audible to me, lasted for three minutes that time, then faded away. About ten minutes later an aeroplane did fly over and I was able to compare the sounds. They were similar, but this time it was definitely outside my head and not inside as before and John was able to hear it too.

After that the sound changed to a high-pitched whistle which I found quite disconcerting, especially during the time when it coincided with a dancing lesson. With that shrill sound in my left ear and the music of the cha-cha-cha in my right, the concentration on my footwork was not too good at that point.

About two months later, in the same room, I was the timekeeper for a Gardeners' Club Quiz and was fascinated to find that during the tea break, when over one hundred people were talking amongst themselves, not only did I have a shrill whistle in my left ear, but the sound of the noise in the room lessened considerably until it sounded more like a whisper. Then as the whistle became quieter and faded away, so the sound in the room rose until it returned to the level it had been before.

* * *

On New Year's Day 1990, after welcoming in the new year at a dance,

155

I had settled into bed at about 2.00 a.m. when I felt a gentle cold movement of air on the left side of my face. This had happened on two occasions before Christmas and though I thought it strange I had not mentioned it to anyone. This time, as before, John was asleep and after a while it stopped, but this one did not slip from my memory as readily as on the previous two occasions and it was on my mind during the next day. Even so, it was a surprise to find that almost forty-eight hours later the same thing was happening again.

I could not describe it as someone breathing gently on me as that would have been warm air. This was icy cold and it only affected the left half of my face. If I had drawn a line down the centre of my forehead, to the tip of my nose and continued to the centre of my chin, the left side was freezing cold and the right side was glowing with warmth.

"Can you feel a draught on the left side of your face?" I asked John who was still awake this time. "No," came the answer. I described what I felt but was assured that I was alone in this. "It's the ghost of Christmas past, come to haunt you," he volunteered.

This time, however, I had timed it. It lasted for three minutes then almost immediately that part of my face was as warm as the other and that was the last time that happened.

* * *

Three times during the year I noticed an unusual smell in the bedroom. Each time it happened just before I went to sleep and on the third occasion I went downstairs to the kitchen to see if I could find something which it resembled. I concluded that night that it was a cross between aniseed and cloves and having made that decision, it stopped. A few weeks later Terri picked some flowers from the garden and brought them into the house. I had instant recognition – it was the scent of carnations.

* * *

One night whilst walking along the road after a meeting, a blue light flashed out from behind a cloud. I sometimes see smaller versions of it in the corner of the bedroom.

Here on several occasions a small black circle with a golden glow around it has moved from left to right across the room and once a black eye-shape, also with a golden glow around it, moved slowly from right

156

to left. This looked to me to be about one inch in length and about half an inch from top to bottom in the centre. Then, as it moved slowly across, it was as if I was told to open my eyes to see whether it was still there. I did – and it was. It continued to the left hand side of the room as I watched it and suddenly disappeared.

On another occasion a very small dumb-bell shape, about four inches long, crossed the room. It was a brilliant white light with the left sphere being much clearer and brighter than the right one. It moved from left to right and was also visible when I opened my eyes. Then as it reached the wall the light faded away and I could see it no longer.

* * *

It is very frustrating when you want to use something and it is not in its usual place. This has happened several times, but always the items have been found and usually in a different room from the one expected. The strangest case of this phenomenon happened on one brilliantly sunny morning as I was about to set off on a shopping trip.

As I have cataracts growing in both eyes I have to wear tinted spectacles, but whenever the sunlight is really bright I also wear an eye-shade. I have an unusually shaped blue transparent one with white spots on, which I have worn for over fifteen years. It always hangs on a hook on the coat rack in the hall and no-one else uses it. On this particular morning it was not there. I spent some time looking for it but to no avail. I did have a spare white one which was rather uncomfortable to wear but in view of the brightness of the light I decided I must make do with that.

When shopping I always take with me several plastic carrier bags folded flat, all inside the outer one. I picked up everything I needed, closed the front door and got into the car where I put the flat carrier bags on to the passenger seat and the white eyeshade on to the back seat.

Arriving in Daventry I found a parking space and decided to put on the white eyeshade. I leaned over to collect it from the back seat and as I did so noticed that my carrier bags were not flat. They were bulky. I picked them up and there inside was my missing blue eyeshade. It definitely had not been there when I started my journey. Was this an example of telekinesis, I wondered. This is the term used for the paranormal movement of objects.

* * *

I have noticed too that sometimes when I read, words or phrases will

157

stand out. Mostly I do not realise the significance of that emphasis but sometime later, perhaps after a phone call or a meeting connected with UFOs, I will find that they have a relevance. My mind is obviously being alerted to those facts.

It was like that when I read *Abduction* I was really looking for a case similar to mine but 1992 kept shouting at me. It was to be over a year later when a phone call from Wales made me realise the significance of that date (Chapter twenty) – and it was nothing to do with our entry into the Common Market!

Here also there was the inclusion of "promised a return visit" which I was quoted as having said (Chapter eight). No reason for that has ever been understood, as when Jenny checked her manuscript it was not there. But had it not appeared in the book, the necessity to understand more about the UFO phenomenon would never have arisen.

* * *

Strange things seem to happen sometimes with regard to electrical equipment belonging to those in contact with UFO witnesses.

On the minus side where contact with me is concerned, one reporter told me that he had written an article about me for a newspaper and had left it on the screen whilst he had his lunch. When he returned to it again it was completely obliterated and he had to write it a second time. That time it was also removed, the screen became a series of crosses. The article had to be written a third time before he was able to use it. Someone, somewhere was obviously not happy with his first two attempts!

Several BUFORA investigators have no explanation as to why tape recorders do not function properly during an interview, yet may work perfectly before and afterwards.

One was using a music centre to record a radio programme on which I was speaking, but just as the interviewer asked me about my sighting there was a malfunction and nothing more was recorded. The equipment has since been checked. All the parts work properly but although taping from records is successful it cannot be done from the radio.

There is no record of the taped hypnosis sessions I had, nor of the two to three-hour interview with another group of investigators although tape recorders were used. The tapes in both cases have disappeared.

But on the plus side, Derrick's computer still works perfectly since I jokingly asked my 'UFO friends' for help (Chapter eighteen). Believe what you will, but these are only a few of the strange and inexplicable tales about electrical equipment malfunctioning when something to do with UFOs is concerned.

* * *

These strange happenings began to occur during 1989 and gradually I came to understand that a new kind of awareness was taking place. I did not know what it was leading to at the time, only that there seemed in retrospect to have been a pattern to it all.

Each of these things happened in groups of five or six, or just as many as were needed to make me realise that each had happened before, to ask myself why and to make a decision to analyse them. Then I was able to accurately describe them when I was attending a function at which there would be people present who could give me an explanation. This was usually at a NUFORC meeting and as soon as I had an answer to that particular phenomenon it stopped and a new one started.

They continued at intervals and gradually I came to wonder whether it could possibly be that in some way I was being tested.

There was the time when every one around me seemed very negative in outlook and sarcastic and this lasted for several weeks. I had read in my horoscope: 'Mars is putting obstacles in your way', and that turned out to be no exaggeration. One day at a meeting I mentioned that 'they' were at it again and that this time it seemed as if it was my patience which was being tested. Whether Mars then went off to upset another group of people I do not know, but from that day onward life returned to normal and I was in happy surroundings again.

I understand now that these are psychic phenomena and it seems that they were a kind of initiative test to see which talents could best be used in the future. At the time I could not envisage the reason for it all as I had no intention of creating for myself a new career in my retirement, but I did wonder.

Perhaps I had proved to be unflappable yet curious when coming into contact with the unknown and perhaps I was endowed with the right amount of patience? Then I wondered if mental agility would perhaps come into it because at one time, when travelling home on a train from a London meeting, I suddenly had the urge to write poetry and by the time I had arrived at Milton Keynes I had composed nine verses.

159

The subject was my close encounter and over the following two days I wrote thirty-three verses covering every detail which I felt it was essential to include. They just flowed from my mind on to the paper and only three of them needed to be altered in some small way at the end. The poem, 'A Strange Experience' is printed on pages 195-199.

Did I pass that test, I wonder? Well, perhaps not, as on another train journey, this time to appear on Tyne Tees Television, I found I was able to describe that also in poetry form ('Food for Thought' pages 199-201).

With Graham and Valerie's encouragement, I became aware that these events were an introduction into an impending change that was to come in my life and which I would not have otherwise understood, and I realised that I was not being tested, I was in fact being trained.

Chapter Twenty-three

A WONDERFUL GIFT

By the time the last decade of the century arrived, my understanding of the UFO phenomenon had increased considerably. Writing this account had meant that I had searched deeply into my subconscious for reasons for that encounter and now I knew that I had answers which satisfied me as to what could have happened. But there was still another surprise in store.

Having by this time met many people who had seen UFOs and many of whom had also had abduction experiences, I was aware that under hypnosis some claimed to have been promised a return visit after a certain number of years had passed, some were subjected to an examination of some kind and many claimed to have been given information which they would not remember for a number of years.

I was finding that I was being asked to speak about my experience quite openly to groups of people not only on the media but at Adult Education classes, BUFORA meetings and at Conferences, and I was told several times by those I had met at ICUR that in these following twelve months I had become much more confident in doing so. The reason for this was that I could now see that there was to be a happy ending to it all.

In many ways I am now very pleased that I never had a second session of regressive hypnosis. It has meant that I have had to find out so many things for myself in my own way and always there has been that little bit of uncertainty which has made the whole exercise so much more exciting.

So, during my fifteen-minute time lapse, was I promised a return visit in ten years' time as some abductees were? If I were then it could have been in the form of a visit to Terri, so as to further arouse my interest in the subject.

Was I subjected to an examination of some kind during that missing time? Obviously, yes. I am sure that the whole episode was of a serious nature and not merely a game. Gary H. has always said that the examination was one of a spiritual kind and that explanation ties in with what is happening to me now.

Also, was I given information which would not come to the fore until after a certain passage of time? This I now believe to be so. Like the 'promised a return visit' in Jenny's book when I found that my quite literal interpretation did not occur, so with this information there was a gradual build-up of knowledge and a getting to know of people who were able to enlighten and encourage me in this development. But it was a surprise visit to a medium, which had been organised by a friend on the 14th February 1990, that caused everything to fall into place.

"You are entering a new pathway in life," I was told, "and you must take advantage of it."

During the hour and a half which I spent with Charles Chapman I learned that I would come into exciting times and that if I did not drive myself too hard I would find that the next year would be a very wonderful one. We talked about pain and how when you have been deep in suffering it puts you on a different level of understanding and strength. Not only do we gain knowledge ourselves, but our fellow beings gain also.

"You are in for a very wonderful year," he assured me and I commented that I now felt fit enough to cope with it. "But do keep yourself within your limitations," he warned.

I had found since the new year began that I was coming into contact with people who were healers and several friends whom I had known for many years were now telling me that they also had the gift.

Valerie had put her hand on mine at a NUFORC meeting and a tingling sensation had come into my fingers. Another friend had put his hands on each side of mine and I found the same thing happening. Then at night time I had been finding that the palms of my hands became very hot and that my fingers tingled as well.

Mr. Chapman told me that in his opinion the greatest form of mediumship is healing and that I would come into mediumship through healing if I chose to do so.

"You will carry out some wonderful healing and see some fantastic results," he said. "There is no achievement in life that can equal that to my way of thinking. The rewards are coming if you go forward now.

Happiness is on your doorstep. It is up to you. You have the gift and it would be rather sad if you did not use it."

I tend to question statements like that. In fact at times I am a real 'Doubting Thomas', but I thought about it a lot and realised how wonderful it would be and how privileged I would feel if it came about.

My thinking time is always at the end of each busy day and as I lay in bed that night I was counting my blessings from the previous twenty-four hours as I always do. My overactive mind seemed not to want to rest and gradually I realised that this was not the only cause for the lack of sleep. I had a dreadful ache from my shoulder blade to below my left elbow and no matter what position I turned to I could get no relief.

In desperation I looked at the clock. It was 2.57 a.m. – nearly three o'clock and I was too uncomfortable to sleep. Suddenly I realised that the centres of the palms of my hands were burning hot and I knew instinctively that I had to use that heat on my arm. I passed my right hand gently along it from fingers to shoulder blade and back again. That terrible ache disappeared and I fell asleep.

The next morning I realised that although my sleeping time had been relatively short, it had been a good one and I felt well rested. Of course I realised that it could have been nothing at all to do with 'healing' myself. I could at that time have been so tired I would have fallen asleep anyway, so I decided not to get too excited about it.

Later that day I visited Rose and Terri and was asked how my day out had gone. I mentioned the suggestion I had received about becoming a healer.

"What is spiritual healing, Nannie?" Terri asked.

I explained that, as I understood it at the time, it was when hands were put on people who were ill and the heat which came into them sometimes cured anything that was wrong with that person, but that if it did not cure it, it would make it feel more comfortable.

The palms of my hands were very hot again and I put my right hand near her left cheek to demonstrate. She assured me that she could feel the heat coming from it.

"My toothache's gone," she said suddenly. I looked at her in surprise and Rose told me that she'd had it for the previous three days. This was something I had not known. The family was going to visit friends for the weekend and they had been worried that she was feeling miserable.

I saw them four hours later. All was still well and when they returned home after three days away I learned that Terri had been her usual happy self. Her toothache had not returned.

Was this a sign, I wondered, to prove to my doubtful mind that it really was possible?

A week later I was out with another friend and told her what was happening to me. I then learned that she too was a healer.

"If you have the power you really must use it", she said, "it is a wonderful gift and you can get so much pleasure from helping to bring comfort to other people."

From then on it became obvious that I was developing an insatiable interest in mediumship and healing. I was conscious of clairvoyant images, some of which I found to have a bearing on a future event. Terri had no more toothache and was convinced that "Nanny had cured it", but I still felt that I had no real proof that I was able to help anyone in this way.

Then I began to find that following visits to sick friends, or when I had physical contact with anyone who was ill, I was feeling very uncomfortable myself afterwards.

"It is because you are thinking healing thoughts towards them," I was told, "and you are taking on their pain. There are ways of avoiding this", and a variety of methods were suggested.

Others were also convinced that I could become a very good healer and did everything possible to encourage me.

"In order to develop, a healer has to practise. Begin by healing friends and relatives," I was advised, "practise on them."

I had to understand also that it was not I who was actually doing the healing, but that I was allowing myself to be used as a channel through whom the healing energy, which came from God, would pass (with the help and guidance of spirit doctors) into the person requiring it.

I was soon to find too that not only friends, relatives and animals would be able to benefit from it, but that I could use it to help myself.

A few days later I had lifted my box of shopping from the car boot in such a way that I pulled a muscle in the lower part of my back. It was a silly thing to do. After all I had suffered with my back over the previous six years, I should have had more sense. But there was no point in being angry about it, I told myself. I would just have to suffer until it got better.

By evening the pain had travelled to my right hip, then as I went up the stairs to bed I could feel it moving down my right leg towards the knee. I began to get worried. In bed my hands were hot and my fingers were tingling. It seemed logical to use this power within them on myself, so I placed both hands on the spot where the pain had travelled to (a very difficult exercise whilst lying in bed) and decided to leave them there as long as I possibly could.

The heat generated was comforting and I found surprisingly that my arms, although in a strange position, did not ache. Every part that my hands were in contact with became hot, even the bed. It was like having a hot pad over my hip and I maintained that position for over fifteen minutes.

The following morning the pain was still there so I had to continue to move gently but at lunchtime it was necessary to put something in the dustbin. As I went to lift the lid my right leg went icy cold just above the knee and this coldness travelled up my leg, into my hip and across the centre of my back to the point where the pain had started. There it changed to a tingling sensation and about two hours later I suddenly realised it had stopped. All the pain had disappeared and did not return. I had realised that I could indeed heal myself.

*　*　*

On Monday 9th July 1990, Douglas and his family were to fly from Luton Airport for a holiday in Spain. The excitement was growing and John had arranged to drive them to the airport.

On the previous Tuesday Rose had lifted a heavy package very awkwardly and twisted her back, collapsing on the floor in agony. She was taken to the doctor who prescribed pain-killers and, giving her a certificate, he advised a week's rest at home and a return visit the following Monday, the day she was due to leave for the family holiday.

She rested as much as possible and on Friday came with me when I went shopping. She looked awful and was obviously in much pain as we slowly walked from shop to shop. Having suffered in the same way myself for so long and it being the cause of my retirement from the Teachers' Centre, I fully understood how she felt. I longed to be able to help her and spoke to one healer friend about it.

"Ask her if we can go and see her tomorrow evening," she said, "and we'll see what we can do."

On the Saturday morning I phoned. Rose was no better. In fact that morning she had slipped on the stairs and twisted her back again. She welcomed the suggestion about the visit and at 7.00 p.m. that evening we arrived.

Rose sat on a stool and I stood behind her. "You will do the healing and I will give you extra power," were my instructions. "Start at the top of her head and your hands will tell you what to do."

My hands were extremely hot. They had never reached that temperature before and I passed them from her head, over her shoulders and down to her waist. Over her right shoulder my hand went icy cold and that was the only reaction I had, but I applied my hot hands first of all over her right shoulder. Rose remarked on the heat she felt.

Then I moved my hands to different parts of her back until after about fifteen minutes the heat lessened and stopped. During all this time her hands were being held also and she was receiving additional power for the healing process. Asked how she felt afterwards she said that it had been like having a sunray lamp on her back. She moved her body and said it was much easier to do so.

I saw her on Sunday morning and she said that her right arm had gone cold a short time before. A reaction – that was good. Something was happening.

On Monday morning, the day of their arranged departure for Spain, she had an appointment at the surgery. I also had to go to pick up some tablets for John and expected to be able to give her a lift home, but she was not there. She was not at home either, nor was she with a neighbour.

On my way to the village shop I saw her walking happily along carrying a bag of shopping.

"Just wait till I turn the car round and I'll give you a lift home," I said. "Have you seen the doctor?"

"No," was her reply. "Yesterday afternoon I realised that the pain had disappeared completely and it hasn't come back, so there's no point in going to the doctor."

That evening the family went on holiday as planned.

Almost two weeks later I was lying on my right side in bed and as I turned over I felt an excruciating pain in the area where my appendix has rumbled on and off since the age of two.

John was going off early the next morning to collect Douglas, Rose and the children from Luton Airport. What an inconvenience this would cause if I really had got appendicitis this time. Each time I moved the pain was intense. My hot hands told me to use them so I lay on my back and placed them over the painful area until they cooled down about fifteen minutes later. Then, as there appeared to be no pain I lay still, not daring to move.

Suddenly there was a strange sensation in that area. There was no pain but a feeling of movement inside me as if organs within were being moved about. I kept very still until it stopped. I felt no more pain.

It was then that I realised that there could be a purpose for these things happening to me – so that I could feel for myself the sensations which others experience when on the receiving end of this wonderful gift of healing.

On their return from holiday we were delighted to hear that there had been no recurrence of Rose's back pain and she returned to work the following day to find that her colleagues had heard about the healing and had expressed great interest in it.

Coinciding with this was the arrival of a letter which gave Terri a date for a hospital visit to have the ninth operation on her ears. She had had the first operation at the age of five and over the years grommets, T-tubes and then bobbins had been inserted, but to no avail.

After the seventh operation it was found to be necessary for her to wear one hearing aid as one ear drum had ruptured. Then after the eighth operation she sadly needed two, having been tested and found to be completely deaf in one ear and with very little hearing in the other.

This time the operation was to remove a bobbin but the surgeon found a polyp in her ear and removed that too. She spent two hours in the operating theatre and I collected her from the hospital about two hours after she had returned to the ward. She had ear drops to apply and was told that providing it felt comfortable she could wear her hearing aids two days later.

For two weeks after the operation Terri stayed with John and me and this time I was in possession of something which I had not had before. I was developing as a healer, and as this is something which complements medical science and in no way can do any harm, I gave her healing every night during her stay.

As before, immediately after her operation her hearing improved, but before it had always deteriorated again rather quickly, usually accompanied by an infection. This time it improved daily until Terri asked for the sound to be turned down on the television set, and on one occasion when she had spent the evening at home she complained that the television had been so loud that it had given her a headache.

Over the years she had taught herself to lip read but now we found that we could also hold a conversation with her if we spoke naturally and stood behind her.

Two weeks after the operation she had an appointment to see the specialist. I sat in the waiting room whilst her mother took her into the consulting room. Not long afterwards Terri reappeared.

"Nannie," she said, her face beaming with pleasure, "*Perfect!*" and she danced off along the corridor.

The reading on her hearing test had never been so high and the specialist had never seen the insides of her ears so dry. She was advised to put her hearing aids in a drawer and use them only if she got a cold and could not hear too well.

Four weeks after the operation Rose remarked that by that time following the previous ones, Terri's hearing had deteriorated back to the level it had been before going into hospital, but that this time her hearing was still perfect. She was also enjoying being able to wash her hair and swim without having to use earplugs and hoped never to need them or her hearing aids again.

All these things happened during a period of five months and proved to me how very worthwhile this kind of work can be.

My confidence grew as I learned more about the subject and I began to find that I experienced differing sensations in my hands from heat to icy coldness, or a tingling in my fingers which reached varying degrees of intensity. The patients experienced sensations accordingly from heat to coldness, or as one person said, "It feels like butterflies inside me."

During one healing session a most remarkable thing happened. It was as if I was actually sitting away from myself to my right side and I could see myself in profile, a black outline. There was a strange feeling suddenly in my own head and I could see a golden ball of healing energy within the outline of my head. This went into my right shoulder and down my arm to the palm of my hand, then into the patient. "That was a clairvoyant vision," I was later told by a healer friend. "Spirit was showing you how they see you when they are working through you."

It was time then to understand about one's aura and I learned that every living body, people, animals and plants, all have an aura or psychic atmosphere. This extends to about nine inches around the body and is variable in both depth and colour according to the health and feelings of the person concerned.

As yet I have not seen an aura but although it is possible to train oneself to do this, only a trained clairvoyant can see the most subtle variations in the colouring. Maybe this skill will develop for me at some time in the future.

1990 turned out to be the most wonderful year of the sixty-two years of my life. At the beginning of it I could never have imagined the new pathway along which I would travel nor how interesting, exciting and rewarding it would turn out to be. Three years later, during a time when I received Spiritual Writings, this particular period of my life was also described in poetry form (*Healing Development*, pages 202-203).

Chapter Twenty-four

DEVELOPMENT CONTINUES

With the support of family and friends I was ready to go forward into this new progression of service to others and I really looked forward to the future. Retirement for me was certainly going to be an exciting and rewarding experience.

Some periods in one's life stand out as being more memorable than others, and around this time I could not help but think back to those euphoric six months during 1989 when everything seemed to go right as well and the possibility of something going wrong seemed completely out of the question.

Entering 1991 it soon became obvious that this was in no way to be a repeat of that heavenly state. Many people, including me, were attacked by a virus and just as we began to feel well it seemed to attack us again. I was fortunate in that it was only with me for five weeks, but there were some who suffered for many months.

It seemed also to be a time when the advice I had been given previously was being changed frequently and I found myself rapidly becoming frustrated and confused. Some of it was also coming through 'third parties' and by the May 1991 NUFORC meeting it had become necessary for me to seek advice from others whom I knew could help. In my own mind I knew what was right, but if negative and destructive thoughts are continually being fed into one's mind then one does, in the end, wonder whether consideration should be given to them or not.

Over the last few years at UFO meetings, and personally, I had made many friends who were following my new development with genuine interest, and on several occasions I was given the opportunity to discuss my confused feelings. Each time I was given reassurance that I really was heading in the right direction. I am truly grateful to those friends for their patience, understanding and support when I needed it most.

From then onward a new positive me emerged and I went forward again having, during the first six months of that year learned much about human nature of all kinds – but even more about myself, and I believe that I am now a much more balanced person because of that experience.

During part of that time I had felt too ill to do any healing apart from helping myself. In any case it would have been unwise to have contact with other sick people in case I passed on the virus to them; so when I received a mysterious message via 'a friend of a friend' telling me that I was to stop contact healing and to concentrate instead on absent healing, I did not question the wisdom of it.

It was most unexpected and did seem to be a strange suggestion but it was something I could do alone. No-one else needed to be involved and my sick friends could still be helped from a distance. I had no idea how to do it, I had never seen it done, but then contact healing is performed differently by each healer, so I decided to work out my own technique. I liked finding out things for myself and in time I had worked out a system which felt right for me.

In the same way as with contact healing my channel had to be opened because I do not heal or cure anybody. That is done by helpers in the Spirit world who can only use their healing skills for the benefit of people on this earth through human channels – and I am one of those channels.

As with contact healing I started with a prayer asking that my channel should be opened and that the healing energy should flow through to those in need of it. I found that my hands got very hot after that and during this time I asked for healing to be given to certain people whom I knew needed help.

Now whether that was right or wrong I didn't know, but during the year I again visited Charles Chapman who had originally told me that I could become a Healer if I chose to do so, and during the time I was with him he asked suddenly, "Do you want to know how your absent healing is going?"

"Well, yes please," I answered.

"You are treating a sick child, aren't you?" he continued, and I explained that it was my grand-daughter who was having problems with her ears.

"Yes," he said, "it's been very successful. Keep it up. It will be very successful."

I had received confirmation that the technique I was using for absent healing was obviously effective and in 1995 she still wears no hearing aids and everything seems normal.

* * *

By this time I had noticed Psychic Events were taking place in the Daventry area and out of curiosity I paid them a visit. There I found that I was on the same wavelength as those displaying their goods and talents.

I talked to everyone willing to do so. I asked endless questions and information flowed which was readily soaked up by my inquisitive mind. Looking back this was the beginning of an understanding about crystals, pendulums, auras, meditation, psychic portraits and other related subjects, all giving me a deeper insight into the pathway along which I now seemed to be confidently travelling.

One purchase I made was of a crystal attached to a piece of twisted wool. It was a pendulum I was told and I was shown how to use it to see the depth of my aura. Later I was to learn other uses for it. For me it swings from side to side for *yes* and in a clockwise direction for *no*. Towards the end of the year I was to find that it could also swing backwards and forwards for *don't know*, though I have never yet had that response from it.

All questions must be asked in such a way as to require a *yes* or a *no* answer which, although it sounds simple, I found to be very tricky at first. I use it for all kinds of things and I find it especially good for telling me the wisest foods for me to eat.

In August 1991 another UFO Conference was held, this time in Sheffield and although I decided not to attend this one because it coincided with John's and my Ruby Wedding Anniversary which was exactly twelve years to the day after my hypnosis session, I was still involved. Prior to the Conference, Philip Mantle did an excellent job in promoting it and I was again asked to tell my story on television and radio, also I was interviewed and photographed for several women's magazines.

After this I was contacted by two people who had read an article in one of the magazines in which the last paragraph read: 'Elsie, who has now discovered a new-found gift of healing, insists: "I do believe that any power I have may well have come from my encounter with the

UFO." ' Each writer had a member of the family who was ill with cancer and they both hoped that I could help.

"Spirit works in strange ways," I had been told before (Chapter eighteen p. 130) and this may well have been another example, for although the article in that magazine, which both had read, had been attributed to two reporters and was full of quotation marks, indicating to the reader that I had given an interview, neither of these reporters nor anyone else from that magazine had contacted me at all.

I felt sure that I could help. I really wanted to, but was not yet clairvoyant enough to see exactly how, so I decided to see if my pendulum would give me some answers.

I held it over the letters and asked a series of questions appertaining to the requests and finally received instructions resulting from those questions. Yes – you can help these people; yes – give absent healing daily; yes – 11 o'clock in the evening will be a convenient time, and so on. I wrote to say that I would help them with absent healing at 11 o'clock each evening and explained what healing was: that it comes from God, that it was not me doing it but spirit helpers working through me and that, as I understood it, you cannot overdose on healing because spirit regulates the dose. We exchanged photographs and at 11 o'clock each evening we were really together.

Sadly, in time both patients died because healing unfortunately cannot prolong life, but it does help towards a peaceful passing at the end. I now have several people on my absent healing list and wherever I am at 11.00 p.m. I find a quiet place and open my channel. My hands get very hot and my fingers tingle whilst the healing is taking place, then when it stops I close myself down. It has become quite a ritual since those letters arrived and the advice I received at the beginning of the year did prove to be sound after all, and because of it I had learned about another type of healing.

* * *

Also during this time it was suggested that I should join two others on a visit to a Healer in another part of the country and that we should all have some healing from him whilst we were there. At the time I could not understand why anyone should think that I needed healing. After all, I had become a Healer myself and had been able to help myself, but I decided to go along with them. It would be an interesting experience to see how another Healer worked.

173

To my surprise this was a Trance Healer. I had never seen anyone in a trance before and did not know what to expect, so I decided that I would wait for my healing until last.

The patient sat on a stool with the Healer standing behind him. A lady with outstretched arms stood by his side. She was later described to me as being the 'Power House' She was giving extra power to the healing process and giving protection to the Healer whilst he was in a trance. The Healer said a short prayer and breathed very deeply, then he spoke. His voice had changed completely. He had been taken over by his Spirit helper who was then in complete control of the situation. I found it fascinating to watch.

When it was my turn and I was in a comfortable sitting position this 'different' voice asked, "And how can I help you, my dear?" Making a quick decision I decided to tell him about the problems I had had with my back; problems which by then I had come to terms with, could cope with, and no longer thought of as problems.

"I had to retire from work about six years ago with spinal spondylosis," I began.

"No such thing," he announced very positively and proceeded to examine my spine.

"And I still have to wear a collar sometimes," I added.

Then I heard what sounded like the slapping of one hand against another, except that it sounded more like a 'crack'. This happened four times altogether, then he told me that I had been involved in a car accident when a young child and that my need to wear a collar was caused not by 'wear and tear' (as my doctor had said) but because of a whiplash injury sustained in that accident.

He asked me if I could recall anything like that happening, and I could. I must have been about seven years old when dad jammed on the brakes of the car and I, sitting in the front passenger seat, had shot forwards towards the windscreen – and screamed. I remember no pain at all, just being told off for screaming.

"Yes, that's right," he said.

My fully relaxed body was then moved in a way in which I would never have thought possible. The top part of me was lifted and twisted around so that I faced 90° to the right, then 90° to the left of the normal sitting position – then it was relaxed. Immediately my head seemed to be lifted off my shoulders and turned in the same way. I cannot remember ever having been able to do that before.

My instructions following the healing, during which I felt no discomfort at all, were to move carefully and to soak for a quarter of an hour in a hot bath containing a handful of sea salt, twice a day for a week, and after each bath to rub Witch-Hazel on my back. This I did do.

On the day after the healing I woke up to find my spine stiff from top to bottom. It was as if I was wearing a corset and had heavy weights on my shoulders. I seemed to have a new upright shape. Then about two days later the stiffness started to wear off a little at a time from my neck downwards, until a week later when the last piece at the base loosened up.

I learned later that my 'spinal spondylosis' was really four displaced vertebrae and that what I thought sounded like 'cracks' was actually the tearing of muscles as each vertebra was realigned. Someone said that I should have stayed in bed for the whole of that first week, but I didn't. I did move very carefully though. I had to, the stiffness in my back made certain of that. Everyone with whom I came into contact said I looked awful. I will admit to it now, though I wouldn't at the time. I felt far from well after that visit but I carried out the instructions to the letter and my back is now very straight and I have not needed to wear my collar since.

Some months later I was given the opportunity to witness the man advertised as 'having been one of Britain's leading Healers for ten years'. We were invited to join Matthew Manning for a 'truly inspirational evening' and to share with him his approach to healing, relaxation and positive living.

This took place at Nene College in Northampton on 30th May 1991 and no fault could be found with that advertisement. The evening was truly inspirational and impressed me immensely.

After an introductory talk about his life up to the time he became a Healer he demonstrated the way he works. The patients were taken from the audience and received their healing from Matthew in a silent room with over 200 people all contributing by thinking healing thoughts at the same time.

A lady with a 'frozen' shoulder could afterwards lift her arm above her head. One with back problems who could only reach her knees could afterwards bend to touch her ankles, and twelve volunteers all deaf in either one ear or both joined hands in a circle. Healing was given to only one of the group and afterwards two of the others also had improved hearing. The patients were told that the healing process would continue during the night and that others were expected to find that their hearing had improved by the following day.

175

Matthew, who travels around the world and has featured in books, articles, television and radio programmes, is well-known for his continuing success in healing patients with cancer and other life threatening illnesses. I learned much that evening which was to be very useful in the future.

* * *

During the year a lot of information about crystals came my way and without realising it I was to find that the information which I absorbed unconsciously would also be useful for healing. Initially it was a time similar to the beginning of 1990 when I seemed to find that many people I met were Healers. Now I was finding that everyone seemed to bring crystals into the conversation.

At one Psychic Event I had looked at crystal clusters and decided to buy one.

"What about this one?" asked the young man pointing to a rather lovely cluster.

"No," I said, "not that one. This is the one that takes my eye", and I bought a short, dumpy one with baby attached. I was to learn later that it was the right one for me. It is said that a crystal chooses its owner and that you will instinctively know which is the right one to have.

Later in the year I attended an Adult Education course on 'Natural Therapies'. This reinforced some of the things which I, by then, was considering to be a normal part of my everyday thoughts and activities.

'Chakra' is a word which I was to find entering my vocabulary. I learned about our outer bodies and came to realise that the chakras are seven energy centres situated along the course of the spine in the etheric body, through which life energies flow.

On one day of the course one practical exercise was to diagnose whether any of the chakras was out of balance. A pendulum was used for this and, if so, certain types of crystal, set in specific positions, were placed on the body above that particular chakra in order to recharge it. At the same time a stress-release exercise was performed on the patient and after twenty minutes the pendulum retested the result. On the occasion I was the Healer, the patient had an imbalance in the area of the heart chakra and after treatment the pendulum confirmed nothing more needed to be done. The patient was well-balanced again.

Since acknowledging that, because of the knowledge I had by then acquired regarding UFOs, a second session of hypnosis would be unwise, it had been suggested to me by many people that meditation could be the answer.

This was a suggestion which was becoming more logical as time passed and I found was also being reinforced by new people I was now meeting.

"A good idea," I was told by one, "sit quietly and empty your mind and let Spirit, your UFOs or whatever, come in." So I developed a programme for meditation and put into practice the points which had been suggested.

Meditation at regular times is recommended and I expected communication of some sort, but still my mind wandered. Then it was encouraging to be told, "When you are meditating you may think that you are sitting doing nothing, but there is a lot going on. Your helpers are working hard to tune in to your vibrations. Theirs are very fast and yours are very slow. They are working to become attuned to you, to bring their vibrations into harmony with yours." Talking to these people I learned about the way Spirit helpers make contact with human channels.

Then during the 'Self-Awareness' section of this course I found confirmation for past efforts. Not only did I find that the meditation which I do alone at home is done satisfactorily, but also during one group meditation exercise, when I lost concentration, I was suddenly aware of a message: "You are expecting too much of yourself – too soon."

How true! This could have been the cause of the frustration and confusion which I had experienced earlier in the year. Also it was a timely reminder of the advice I had received that day in Rugby from Charles Chapman: "Do keep yourself within your limitations."

Chapter Twenty-five

MORE SURPRISES

In 1978 I had suggested to a caller at my front door the possibility that 'they' might invade the earth and on Radio Leicester in 1980 'they' were referred to as possibly being people from another planet. How much further has our knowledge of this phenomenon progressed since that time?

As regards life on other planets I have always been of the opinion that if man is capable of landing on the moon, and we know that he is, then how can we say for certain that there is no life on other planets – or that the inhabitants of those planets are incapable of visiting ours? Most would agree that if this should be so then these visitors must be of a higher intelligence than we are, if only because of the manoeuvrability of the craft which we assume to be theirs.

In recent years much more UFO activity has been reported and more is expected in the future. The size and variety of shapes of corn circles, another phenomenon leading to much speculation, has warranted a great deal of media coverage. In fact the circles can no longer be assumed to be seen as circular. They now comprise lines, spurs and circles in a variety of sizes and positions, often altogether as one unit. In 1990 there was one which was dumb-bell shaped.

In August of the following year the opportunity arose which gave Reg Pinckheard, a fellow member of NUFORC, and me the hope that we could assist researchers of corn circles to find an answer.

I was awakened that morning by a phone call from Reg. He had read in our local weekly newspaper that a corn circle had been found in a field near Daventry. One of the first people to notice it was a young man from Badby and Reg arranged for us to speak to him before we visited the circle.

It had appeared during the night of the previous Sunday and was in a field alongside the A361 road between Byfield and Chipping Warden, at the crossroads to Aston-le-Walls. Following these instructions we found the field and walking along the tramlines through the ripened wheat we found ourselves in the circle.

Neither of us had seen a real one before but we had taken with us a few things which might be useful in our investigations. Reg had balls of string, a knife and a compass. I took a tape recorder, camera, my pendulum and a crystal. Neither of us knew what to expect apart from what we had seen in newspapers and on television, but we both obviously hoped for something.

Knowing that strange things can happen with equipment in this kind of situation, Reg's first task was to ascertain whether his compass would work properly, but it did not deviate from its normal direction. The points N, S, E and W were positioned in the circle, then using the string and a tape measure we found the measurements to be 45 feet 9 inches from N to S and 45 feet 6 inches from E to W. There was a flattened square of corn which was not quite in the centre of the circle. It was 26 inches square, 26 inches being the height of the crop, and was on the eastern side of the central point with the remaining corn rotating around it in an anti-clockwise direction.

On that day I had no knowledge of crystals and had taken mine with me not knowing quite what to do with it. I decided that I would hold it in my hand and walk around the circle in an anti-clockwise direction. A crystal to me feels very cold and so it was when I started at the southern point, but as I passed point E it was becoming warm. By the time I was halfway round the circle my hand and fingers were tingling and I felt a pulsating sensation from the crystal. This sensation continued until the circle was completed.

Then I walked towards the centre. There the crystal was really hot. This was a new feeling to me. I did not know why. The palm of my hand down to my wrist was also very hot and there was a tingling sensation in my first and middle fingers and the pulsating continued. I checked the heat from the crystal on my cheek. Every part, the base, the flat faces and the point were all very hot.

Next I used the pendulum. I walked in the same direction around the outside of the circle but this time I stopped at various points to see what the pendulum would do. I asked it no questions.

On points N, S, E and W there was a strong clockwise swing but between each there was no reaction at all. The pendulum hung limply. Going towards the central point there was a strong side-to-side swing. If it was saying *no* at points N, S, E and W and *yes* in the centre we had no idea what would be the question to ask in order to produce such answers.

The young man who had first noticed this corn circle had described his feelings on entering it as those of happiness, disbelief and wonder at the swirling of the corn. After our investigation and experiments we admitted that we had no feeling of upliftment at all, perhaps because we knew it was there and had not come across it by accident as he had. But we did agree that it was a marvellous experience and that we were fortunate to have been able to visit it.

Driving home it became obvious that a headache was developing and soon after I had a tightening sensation around my head and it felt as if the top was becoming inflated like a balloon. I became very, very tired and slept soundly for nearly an hour.

I woke up feeling elated and this euphoric state lasted from then right through to the end of the following day. Thirty-six hours after our visit Reg described it as "a supportive experience in some way endorsing oneself." We both felt we had been given something, a kind of inner strength and agreed that often, what at the time manifests itself as a casual experience, registers later as something which has much more relevance. We were both delighted to have seen that crop circle and it is an experience which neither of us will forget.

No-one as yet knows what causes these in our fields. Some think the answer comes from above and has either an extraterrestrial or an atmospheric cause, whilst others are equally sure that the answer will be found below ground.

Perhaps visitors from other planets, if they really do exist, know something of the make up of our world which we have yet to learn and these are their ways of bringing to our notice the fact that there is concern by them for the future of our planet? Perhaps these methods are being used at present to bring to our attention the need for that concern and to make us think about our own future?

Of course the different observations made and the different explanations given to these strange events will be interpreted in a variety of ways, each taking into account the listener's or reader's own interest and understanding of the subject.

The time for us to know the truth may not yet be right. A more spiritual change in our way of thinking may be required before it can happen.

* * *

During the evening of 27th September 1990 I had been discussing healing, clairvoyance and clairaudience with a friend. We had meditated together and she then introduced me to something new – automatic writing.

I had heard it mentioned at one NUFORC meeting but did not understand, then towards the end of that meeting it was suggested that we should try it as the speaker had found his own efforts to be "interesting". This I had done two or three times, but on each occasion the only marks on the page were scribbles which meant nothing. They were neither legible nor recognisable pictures so, although I was fascinated by what I had heard about it, at that time I put those efforts aside. On this particular evening together we had tried again.

My friend, who had successfully received information before, did so again and was satisfied that the message she received was genuine. My results were as before, just scribbles – but the only control I had over the exercise was the holding of the pen. The movement of it had been out of my control.

That evening I had received more helpful information to add to my ever increasing knowledge of the subject and as I drove home I was thinking everything through, until I came to the point where I had driven under that dumb-bell shaped object in November 1978.

It was 10.15 p.m. and no moon or stars were visible, when I suddenly became aware of a brightness in the sky to my right and looking in that direction I was able to see what I took to be the fourth moon just forming below a line of three others. Each was below the one above and where each joined there was what appeared to be a narrow strip of cloud crossing in front – a formation of three narrow lace-like strips of cloud.

Assuming that there would have been a full moon that night and that it had been reflected against the clouds, I continued to drive along the A5. Then I looked at it again. This time the four 'moons' were squashing downwards and were becoming pear-shaped. There was a brightness in the sky surrounding this and other cloud formations were clearly visible. Then, as I looked, it grew what appeared to be a tail from the bottom out to the right and resembled a small child's drawing of a cat.

At the top of the hill, now off the A5, I could see it again. It was by this time a much larger orangey-yellow ball of light with two tails, one on each side forming the shape of a boomerang – a ball of light sitting on a boomerang.

Continuing my journey, I reached the corner of the village where I had before found myself sitting in complete darkness and again I was able to observe a further change in shape as I looked between the farm buildings. It was as if it had rolled over and the 'boomerang' was pointing to the right, rather like an arrowhead. Here I did stop my car to look at it. In fact I reversed around the right-angled bend in the road and was able to position it in relation to the village of Upper Stowe.

I drove on past the church and there it was again but this time the boomerang-shaped part of the light had disappeared completely. It was just a very large ball about the size of a large orange in comparison to the moon which I had estimated would have been about the size of a two pence piece. The three narrow strips of cloud were still across it.

In the time that it took to drive into the garage and close the garage door, the whole thing had disappeared. It was 10.20 p.m. and the sky was completely dark. I could see no moon, stars or clouds. What I had originally thought to be the moon was no longer there.

John and I discussed this strange phenomenon. By then I knew that anything unusual which is seen in the sky is initially classed as a UFO. I also knew that UFOs came in a variety of shapes and sizes, including boomerang shapes, but I knew as well that about 95% of all sightings do have a scientific explanation. So when he suggested it could have been caused by refraction, the bending of rays of light as they pass through substances of varying density, it seemed like a logical answer, but there were still things I needed to know about it.

The following evening I was only able to see the moon as it rose and noticed that it was only half visible. Later the cloud was so dense that again no moon or stars could be seen and I began to wonder whether the light on the previous night could have caused a half moon to distort to such a degree that it could have been observed as a full circle, or indeed four full circles.

During the following week the weather changed and I was able to observe the shape and position of the moon in the sky. It had by then almost reached a full moon size and was high in the sky at the relevant time. Also, when travelling along the same road at that time I was able to see that it was positioned high on the left-hand side of the A5 whilst the 'lights' had been low down on the right-hand side.

Research which followed showed that no-one else had seen this phenomenon. It was something the like of which I had never witnessed before and it was a spectacular sighting which left me with a feeling of wonder and speculation.

Was it perhaps the 'return visit' that Jenny mentioned in her book? Maybe, but whilst some are certain that refraction of the light caused it, others are equally certain that it did not.

The one thing that is certain though is that after that experience, that same night, I was able to do legible automatic writing. At first I did lots of letter patterns the same as those I had used when teaching the Infants to write in school, then words like '*Elsie welcome*', and I learned that my Spirit Guide's name was Mukelib and that he would be with me on Thursday evenings, the night we did meditation and discussed my development as a Healer.

The Thursday routine continued, also the automatic writing. Some of the messages were helpful but some were confusing and sometimes it seemed as if there were jokers around, though sometimes they had a strange way of forecasting an event.

One message told me that I would meet a man at a certain dancing class who would have a bad back, that I would give him some healing and that he would get better immediately. What actually happened after that class was that a lady who had just had the plaster removed from her broken arm was still feeling some pain in her wrist. We talked about healing, which she had done herself in the past and I demonstrated on her arm the way in which I worked. She said it felt much more comfortable afterwards.

That same week another friend had a painful leg and asked for some healing, which I gave. Just below the knee she said she could feel the heat going up her leg. Over her ankle she could feel a sharpness which she described as being like a needle giving an injection at that point. When I left she said that her leg was less painful and the following morning she phoned to say that all the pain had gone. The automatic writing which came following this had read: 'One day you will be a great healer'. I do hope so, the relief from pain and suffering which patients feel after receiving healing is the greatest reward anyone could wish for.

Four weeks after the automatic writing had begun, with the

information about Mukelib, I was instructed to stop. It said that I would be contacted in my sleep instead.

At fifty minutes past midnight on Monday, 29th October I awoke to see a large ball of orangey-yellow light in the sky. It was in the same position as the previous light formations had been and was as if it was showing me what had happened whilst I was putting my car into the garage on that occasion. The only difference was that the previous ball of light had three narrow strips of cloud across it, whereas this time the top left-hand corner had a diagonal straight edge cutting off that area of the light.

As I watched it, during about two minutes, it moved straight downwards in the sky behind layers of cloud until it was below the horizon, leaving a reflection of orange light on the underside of the cloud layers above it. Stars were clearly visible in the sky that night but I could see no moon.

I returned to bed and later when nearly asleep I turned over. There, in front of me, a face appeared. It was a dark-skinned, heavily-lined face, that of a North American Indian. My immediate reaction was to ask, "Mukelib, is that you?" There was no reply either spoken or in my mind and the face faded away. That evening there was also a green glow around a pyramid which is on a shelf in the bedroom.

The next night I was able to see that the moon at the same time was in a position much higher in the sky than the orange ball of light had been on the previous night.

Since that time I have described these events, which to me seem to be linked, to many groups of people and have received a variety of suggestions.

One interested listener asked if I knew anything about Egyptian symbols and said there was one which is a ball shape with a wing on each side of the base. My description had made her think of that which she said is a sign of protection. Another person explained that the circle is a spiritual symbol representing perfection and that if it has wings it symbolises a heavenly messenger spreading divine knowledge.

A third person also thought it was spiritual. He said that he felt it was my own spiritual symbol and would account for the fact that no-one else appears to have seen it.

Two comments by healers after hearing about it were: "The Spirits work in strange ways", and: "They get up to all kinds of tricks you know."

One day I may find an answer which satisfies me completely, perhaps one which ties all three sightings together. Until then the first is still definitely classed as a UFO (an Unidentified Flying Object) and the series of light formations I prefer to think of as UAP (Unidentified Atmospheric Phenomena) all in my mind unable to be explained adequately as yet. But who knows, maybe the answers are just around the corner.

Chapter Twenty-six

MY WAY AHEAD

After my visit to Charles Chapman, when my surprise at the revelation about becoming a healer had subsided a little, and I began to understand the implications of it, I told several of my friends about the choice I seemed to have regarding my future.

Most understood this no more than I did at the time but they were happy for me because I was happy about it myself. Everyone followed my development with interest and as I went forward I received much encouragement and advice. Most of this was helpful and positive, but one of the saddest pieces of advice which I was given was that if I did choose to become a healer, I would have to be prepared to give up my many other interests, as healing would be a full-time job. "You won't have time for UFO meetings, dancing, or any of the other things you spend a lot of time doing now," I was told.

"What a strange thing to say," I thought at the time, but I said nothing, just thought a lot! I have always felt that one of the nice things about thoughts is that, unless they are spoken, no-one else knows what they are.

I looked around at the healers I knew, ordinary people like me, some doing everyday jobs, some retired, many happily married with families; all doing healing as and when required in their own homes, the patient's home, or in a Healing Group. Each was a very happy person with a sense of humour and a warm, welcoming smile making everyone immediately feel at ease.

It took no time at all to decide what to do with that piece of advice. After all, healing is a service to others and what a dull person I would become if I had no other interests.

So I am continuing my lifestyle exactly as before, only now I have another new interest to add to the rest. Those of us who become healers come from all walks of life. There are no barriers and the most interesting thing I have found, now that news of this has penetrated the UFO world, is that many other abductees are also finding that they too have become, or are becoming, healers like me.

Towards the end of the year, whilst discussing healing with two friends, it was suggested that I should become a Probationer Member of the National Federation of Spiritual Healers. Sponsorship was offered which I gratefully accepted and on 25th October 1991 my membership application was officially confirmed, then in May 1993 I became a Healer Member of the Federation.

* * *

During that time I met and teamed up with another healer and in August 1992, Audrey Hooker and I formed our own group working at her home on Thursday evenings. We each have a different style when healing and complement each other well. We have also noticed the potential in some of our patients to become healers themselves and have encouraged them to do so, and as we all continue to develop we find we also use crystals and pendulums in our healing sessions.

I had used my pendulum before on many occasions (Chapter twenty-five) but it was Audrey who suggested that I might like to use it to help in some research she and her neighbours planned to do in an entirely different direction from any in which I had used it before, and without being given any details I agreed. Arriving at the appointed time on a lovely summer evening a few days later it was suggested that I should dowse in her back garden, and not knowing what to expect I did so. I asked no questions. I didn't know how to word them but watched the reactions I got from the pendulum. I found that an area from top to bottom of the garden was obviously different from that at the sides and Audrey told me then that I had confirmed what she already knew. I had marked out a ley-line at the back of her home.

Just outside the village are the overgrown remains of an Anglo Saxon Castle and Audrey felt that 'her' ley-line could possibly go in that direction so about a month later I went with her and her neighbours Peter and Sue to the site. As I had been able to plot the ley-line in her garden, this exercise extended the possibility that it could be traced further.

The three of them held crystals as we trudged through the undergrowth and they all noted the responses they received from them as we walked. Audrey, who is very sensitive to a crystal's reactions, is also psychic and was able to deduce the original use of the many areas we covered, with the back-up of answers from questions put to my pendulum. Here too I came across something most unexpected whilst clambering along the moat. There ahead of me was a fallen tree crossing my path, exactly as had been described by Graham Phillips prior to my hypnosis (Chapter four) and here I was with the real-life situation as he had described it. This one was a very dead tree and would have been unsafe to clamber over. It had fallen in such a way too that it was impossible to climb over or to creep under it. All possibilities being taken into consideration on that day, I had to climb out of the moat and find a way through the live undergrowth in order to continue in the direction I was following whilst plotting a ley-line.

I could see why I had remembered that question which was asked whilst I was being psychoanalysed but what a roundabout journey I'd had over fourteen years in order to check my answer!

One of the most interesting discoveries was a spot at which Audrey's body temperature also indicated a site of some importance. Also with us was Sue and Peter's dog, one which had received healing from Audrey. About a month before this he had been near death but on that day he was bounding happily through the undergrowth and nosing into badger setts. As we stood at this particular spot questioning the pendulum, Sue realised that her dog had joined us. At that moment we found ourselves, quite unintentionally, standing in a semi-circle, absolutely still with the dog between Sue and me, also facing inwards, his nose forward and not issuing a movement or a sound. It was as if we all realised (including the dog) that we were standing in a very reverential area.

Audrey's questioning and sensitivity revealed that we were standing over a point where an altar had stood. Suddenly her body temperature changed and she felt that a spirit from that time had joined her, and this was confirmed by the pendulum. Then it returned to normal. The spirit had gone – and so had the dog.

As well as the natural mounds of a castle and the moat we were able to find two ley-lines which crossed at the site of the castle (one on the outer edge we estimated to be approximately 11 metres wide). We also found an underground stream, so deduced that there would have been a plentiful supply of water when the castle was in use.

To the side of the castle was a very flat squareish shaped field which we assumed to have been a parade ground. This was also confirmed.

We all felt that this had been a most interesting and rewarding exercise and we agreed to revisit the area at sometime in the future so that we can map the castle and more accurately plot the points of interest.

Following this, I experienced the same feelings that I had after my visit to the corn circle (Chapter twenty-five). After a really good night's sleep, I felt invigorated as if my batteries had been recharged.

The use of my pendulum on that day ensured that we had a very informative visit with a glimpse into history. A few weeks later whilst walking through Church Stowe I realised that it was possible for my pendulum to also throw some light on to the future.

The parish of Stowe-IX-Churches is reputed to be on a ley-line and the village church in Church Stowe is dedicated to St. Michael. About 100 metres from this church is the spot where my abduction took place. I wondered whether this could in any way relate to a ley-line and I felt an urgency to find out.

On a map of the area I drew a straight line from the castle site to that point in Church Stowe. I dowsed there and found it was on a ley-line. Then on the map I extended the line I had drawn and found that it also crosses the road on the outskirts of the village at the point where the electrics of my car behaved irrationally.

Over the years I have come into contact with many people who are much more informed on this subject than I am and I have put this theory to some of them. All have assured me that this is so – that UFOs do use energy lines and that in other countries this has also been tested. UFO abductions have happened on ley-lines.

My inquisitive mind now wonders whether these energy centres are 'fuel stops' and did I just happen to be in the right place at the right time on that day for the abduction to take place? I am sure that sounds a bit far-fetched to some readers, but when you cannot account for a certain period of time in your life, any possibility is worth considering.

The introduction to the use of a pendulum had opened many doorways and I began to find it a useful thing to carry with me. Obviously it is not wise to rely on it exclusively as it is important to develop one's own intuition about things. *Listen to your inner self* is good sound advice which I pass on as I begin to recognise that this is now happening to me.

* * *

In 1992 it became necessary to make a visit to the specialist in order to have my cataracts examined. It was in 1974 when they were first diagnosed and the vision in my right eye had become quite hazy. He confirmed that they were very slow-growing and needed no further examination from him for another twelve months and that, I felt, gave me time to explore other complementary therapies.

During the Adult Education Course entitled 'Natural Therapies' I had heard about Electro-Crystal Therapy and the encouraging results with reference to cataracts, so I started a course of that treatment in which other types of therapies viz – reflexology, meditation and contact healing all played a part.

At the Healing Group I attended I received healing too, but what amazed me most of all was that whilst sending out absent healing to others I also received healing on my right eye, the one with the more advanced cataract.

This did not happen at every session, but when it did I felt a slight discomfort in that eye, sometimes accompanied by a feeling of swelling within the eye, a very light touch on the eyeball or an itching on the eyelids, but each time there was a build-up of fluid under the eyelid. These healing sessions lasted for anything from five to twenty-five minutes, then the reaction stopped and everything was back to normal. This was something which I had neither asked for nor expected, hence the surprise when it first happened, and I had to be reminded that – "As ye sow, so shall ye reap."

I continued the treatment for a year and then returned to the hospital where I was told that there had been no further development in the cataracts, and it was suggested that I should return in another year when I would probably be discharged.

During this time I continued with the healing and also visited another Trance Healer who, whilst I was with him, treated my arthriticky big toes. When, in June 1994, I returned to the hospital, I was told – "Your cataracts are still there but they appear to have stopped growing. You obviously have great faith in alternative therapies. Keep on with them. We'll discharge you now and you needn't come back to see us again unless your sight deteriorates noticeably."

I told the Healer on my next visit. "It won't," he said – and I belive him.

Six months later, whilst continuing with the healing, it became necessary for me to visit the optician again. The sight in my right eye had improved by two points and in my left eye by one point. My lenses had to be reduced in strength.

* * *

My involvement with the media continues. John Spencer's book *The UFO Encyclopaedia* was published and included an account of my sighting. I was later asked to accompany him to Pebble Mill in Birmingham to help promote on BBC Television, both that and the then impending ICUR Congress in Sheffield.

But of all my contacts with the media the most unexpected one, and the most exciting, was that which enabled me to complete the programme I had been following in order to fully regain my confidence in travelling alone. A voice on the telephone informed me that a programme which was being prepared would include a section on UFOs.

"We understand that you have seen one?" I was asked.

"Yes," I replied.

"And that you would be happy to talk about it."

"Yes, I would," I said.

"Then if we fly you up to Glasgow would you come and tell us about it up here?"

Did she say *fly?* I wondered. Yes, I had not imagined it and on the prescribed day I flew from Birmingham Airport to join Howard Blum, an American author, and Jenny Randles on the set of 'The Garden Party' programme on BBC Scotland Television. Howard was promoting his book *Out There* and Jenny hers and Paul Fuller's *Corn Circles*. I was there to relate my own UFO experience and to do that I had flown alone for the first time in my life – and I felt great!

I am still being asked to speak to groups of people. The audiences are so varied and their interests so different that, although I have only one story to relate, audience participation brings out different aspects of interest and no two meetings are exactly the same.

For the Public Speaking side of my life I give credit to the members of the newly-formed NUFORC group. It was they who encouraged me to speak about it first at their meeting, and since then I have spoken to groups as varied as the Japanese school-children and members of a Ladies British Legion Group.

In May 1991 I did the BUFORA Lecture in London having spoken previously at the International Congress for UFO Research and the Sheffield Conference. In Yorkshire, I also joined the speakers on an Adult Education Course about UFOs, and in Northamptonshire I did the 'UFO Spot' in three courses entitled 'Explaining the Unexplained', 'Exploring the Supernatural' and 'Mysterious Northamptonshire'. In January 1995 I have been asked to give an update on the developments of the last three years at BUFORA's Regional Meeting in Northampton.

I have received questionnaires from people I have never met asking for help in research they were doing into a person's reactions following a traumatic experience. They were interested in the ways in which I had handled, amongst other things, other people's ridicule and the sensationalism of the media. These have been a help to me also as I have had to delve deeply into my subconscious for answers.

A radio programme on the subject of UFOs and covering the above aspects was researched by Penny Lawrence and entitled 'The Ufologists'. This has since been broadcast on Radio 4. I had several interviews for this when Penny and I met at UFO conferences, meetings and at home.

Students preparing theses have attended meetings to which I have been invited, in order to gather more information and to get a first-hand account from a UFO witness. Postgraduates from Leicester University, studying for a Certificate in Psychology, listened intently to me in March 1992, asking searching questions, and many offered suggestions as to the reasons for it all. I returned home from that evening with more possible answers to consider.

Having been a teacher, I suppose this is a natural progression into retirement and I enjoy it very much. I have the usual visual aids, the slides Derrick did for me and the OHP transparancies as well. My story is unique and because of the intimate knowledge which I possess, I am the only person in the world who can relate it with understanding.

My mind is still open to all possibilities and as that air of mystery lingers on it continues to intrigue me.

*　　*　　*

At 11.00 p.m. on the 4th October 1991, I was sitting comfortably at the end of the telephone taking part in a phone-in programme for Radio South Coast. In the Portsmouth Studio were John Spencer and Bob Digby. Bob is a former Chairman of BUFORA and was then the Chairman of ICUR.

I had related the details of my UFO encounter and expected to be cut off as in previous radio programmes, but there was a pleasant surprise in store. The link was extended to forty minutes.

John and Bob discussed not only my sighting, but the way it had broadened out to a much wider subject involving other facets not to do with UFOs but which stemmed from the same event.

John also explained how a UFO encounter experienced by an American lady, Katheryn Howard, was so similar to my own, though we came from very different backgrounds and had never met. "The correlation in the stories is quite high," he said. "It is quite incredible."

Bob spoke of a number of BUFORA videos which were being planned for research purposes and would portray the serious side of the subject. I agreed to be one of the subjects of study and 'Penetrating The Web' was made in 1993. He said that what I had described was not the conventional type of object and there was no doubt in his mind that it was something highly unusual for which they do not have a satisfactory explanation. He was also impressed by the fact that I have never made an exotic claim for it and described me as "a credible observer of the incredible".

'The most spectacular sighting in the Midlands' was its description in a newspaper all those years ago and I could never have imagined that interest in it would develop to such an extent as the years passed.

For nearly sixteen years I have tried to find an explanation for what that object was and how such an enormous and solid-looking craft could have been stationary in that position above the road. The question uppermost in everyone's mind is still whether or not I did see an enormous, grey, dumb-bell shaped object above the A5 at Weedon on that evening in November 1978. I know that I did, but was it physically real, and if not, why not?

Towards the end of the programme, I was asked what I thought had actually happened to me as I was driving home that day, what it was that created the lights and gave me the tight feeling around my head, and had subsequently changed my life. What did I now believe to be the cause of it? – and because of my own research and my new way of thinking the answer I gave was that it could have been a psychic experience as no-one else on that busy road had reported seeing it. I have always felt that it was there for me (as were the other light formations I witnessed twelve years later).

The last question I was asked was: "Why do you think whoever, or whatever it was, picked you?" and I found myself replying, "I couldn't say. I have no idea at all but I really would like to know", which according to John was the reply of a "credible person, one who is still questioning, still uncertain and has her feet planted firmly on the ground".

Nearly three years after that broadcast, I am involved in a lifestyle which I had not known existed and could not have envisaged at that time. I continue to talk to groups about that experience and the change in my way of life (I believe) because of it. I am still questioning and still uncertain. Each time I find an answer which I can accept, another question appears.

I thoroughly examine each suggestion offered to the best of my ability, using the knowledge and understanding of the subject available to me at the time. Some have been straightforward and logical, others have seemed extraordinary and beyond belief, but I have not discounted any. We do not yet understand the phenomenon so we cannot know exactly what life has in store for us in the future.

In view of what has happened to me during the last four years, I feel that consideration could be given to the possibility that it *may* have been my first experience of clairvoyance. I wonder? But perhaps not, because there were physical effects also. The electrics of my car were interfered with and control of it was taken out of my hands. I was monitored and manipulated as were the natural light and the time on that particular day. Then later there was a possible corroboration from the sighting at Preston Capes.

But there is also this possibility. Was I given a glimpse into another dimension, and because of the new spiritual understanding I have today do we, the UFO witnesses, have an advantage over everyone else? Perhaps there is someone, somewhere who will later be able to prove the credibility of this point. It would be an interesting piece of research.

I feel that the time is not yet right for us to have a complete understanding concerning these things we refer to as UFOs and aliens, even after more than forty years of research. Undoubtedly, the future will reveal more, then the predictions I have heard and the opinions of the people I have met will be proved to be right or wrong.

Also as time passes UFO researchers will continue to investigate new lines of enquiry and it will be interesting to see whether or not the UFO witnesses really do prove to be the ones who have all the answers.

I *know* they will, for as my mediumship develops I receive, through spiritually inspired writings and drawings, much relevant information – and my clairvoyant friends see what they affectionately describe as 'two little spacemen' with me. My contact with space continues.

A national newspaper once described me as a 'victim' about to 'warn of a mind-blowing threat to the earth' because, it claimed, I had been 'hunted by a UFO' (Chapter nineteen). I was *not* 'hunted' on that day in November 1978. I was *selected* by Spirit *to serve* humanity by spreading the *truth* – and so were the other UFO Witnesses.

POEMS

This poem was written following the second Witness Support Group Meeting in London (April 1990).

A STRANGE EXPERIENCE

A celebration lunch
One late November day
Ended in a wholly
Unexpected way.

Goodness – whatever's happening?
A tightening sensation I feel
Around my head – I'm going to faint.
What an end to a lovely meal!

Suddenly it's over –
No faint, no fuss, I'm fine.
That feeling's soon forgotten
In the brilliant sunshine.

Back in the Teachers' Centre
That afternoon soon goes.
At 5.15 I leave for home
For a more relaxing pose.

It's been a really lovely day,
Blue sky and sunshine too.
The wispy clouds begin to form.
My car behaves well too.

At the traffic lights in Weedon,
Turn on to the A5
What's this I see ahead of me?
How do I stay alive?

The brilliant lights of red and green
Are not a crashing plane.
It's dumb-bell shaped and stationary.
What's this? Am I insane?

I hope I'm not, but what is there
One hundred feet above the ground,
Grey, smooth and plastic looking
And not the slightest sound?

I go along the busy road
And under it I drive.
I feel compelled to stop and look
But this would not be wise.

Turning at the top of the hill
I get a bird's eye view.
It's still there, it winks at me.
I wonder what to do.

I continue my journey
Along that country lane.
The green light goes on flashing
So speed I try to gain.

But now, what's this? My car slows down
Although it's in third gear.
I change to first, thinking the worst
But there's no need to fear.

It starts again and travels on
Along a tree-lined road.
In third again, the fault has gone.
(The end of the episode.)

But there's more. It's all gone dark.
The daylight's disappeared.
Road, buildings, trees and car
Not visible. How weird!

Where am I now? I cannot see.
I don't know what to do.
But look – a circle of bright, white light
Is offering me a clue.

I'm by the farm gate in Church Stowe.
I've travelled round a bend.
How I managed to do that
I cannot comprehend.

Lights flash in semi-circles
Around my stationary car.
I sit in darkness watching them
And wondering what they are.

And from wherever do they come?
They do not have a beam.
Completely circular are they all.
Extremely strange they seem.

Suddenly it's light again,
The darkness disappears.
I see I'm further along the road
Now daylight reappears.

I find my car is in third gear
As normally I drive
Towards the church and round the bend –
Lucky to be alive!

Whilst apparently sitting in darkness
I've travelled one hundred yards.
I did not stop or start my car.
Who did? It's on the cards

That this was by remote control.
I certainly don't know how.
Some mystery being must have helped,
But from where, and why, and how?

I travel home normally
As on any other day,
But find my journey over all
Takes twice as long that way.

It should have taken fifteen minutes.
It's taken half an hour.
What really happened in that time
When my car lost all its power?

I look out of the window
And see a flashing light.
It's yellow this time and going away.
Part of the illusion? Perhaps I'm right?

We talk about my sighting, when
Suddenly – after our meal,
Another tightening sensation
Around my head I feel.

It's just the same as the one before
When having lunch, I felt
As if I'd faint – but as before
It's gone. A blow not dealt.

I wonder now where to find
Explanations for it all.
I decide to tell everyone I meet
Hoping for answers – not too "tall"!

"Oh, that's a UFO," I'm told.
"What's that?" is my reply.
"You ought to tell somebody",
But who, and how – and why?

BUFORA is the group I need
Their investigators are cool.
They listen and interview sensitively
And record without ridicule.

My *close encounter* now I know
Is one of the *fourth kind.*
I was *abducted* in the time I lost.
For what reason? I've yet to find.

But there it is. The years have passed
Since 1978.
Others I've met have tales to tell
About a similar fate.

And all of us are hoping
That in the time to come
The *reason* for such experiences
Will be a *very special* one.

*This poem was written on the train, travelling to take part in a 'Late &
Live' programme on Tyne-Tees TV.*

FOOD FOR THOUGHT

I'm on Northampton station.
The passengers, we wait
To board the train. Then off we go
On time. It wasn't late.

In the train we travel.
Along the line we go
Through villages, towns and countryside
Either fast or slow.

Trees of all descriptions
Enhance the landscape fair.
The beauties of our countryside
We take for granted. There

Are bushes, fields and hedgerows
In varying shades of green
Complementing gardens
In town and country seen.

Some fields are changing colour
As crops ripen in the sun.
The sheep and cows together graze,
At peace with everyone.

The children with their books and pens,
On platforms they select,
Wait for trains to come and give
Their numbers to collect.

We're not the only transport
On the move today,
Cars and buses and motorbikes
Are going on their way.

Aqueducts and viaducts
In stately splendour stand
Over meandering waterways
Which calmly cross the land.

The narrowboats look splendid
Along the side of the line,
As on canals they went their way –
Clean, colourful and fine.

They carry goods and people
As slowly as they will.
How leisurely they travel,
As if the time stands still.

Buildings tall and handsome
Against a blue skyline
Stand out, with chimneys of all shapes.
The scenery is so fine.

Durham Cathedral we've passed by
And York Minster too.
The Garden Festival's in full swing
At Gateshead – a splendid view.

So what's inspiring all of this?
Six hours in a train.
This time I'm travelling northwards.
I'm on the tele again.

That UFO's responsible
For my appearances
On tele and the radio –
And even on a quiz.

To 'Tell the Truth' I had to do
Whilst others had to lie,
Pretending they were really me,
The panel to deny

The chance of winning on that day.
It was enormous fun.
I really did enjoy myself.
Now it's time for another one.

Seven hours ago did I leave home.
The sun was shining too.
But now the rain is pouring down
I'll probably get wet through.

But still it's all in a good cause.
More people will soon know
What happened to me on that day,
And from them thoughts will flow.

They'll wonder what it was and why
It should have chosen me.
The one thing they will certainly have
Is 'Food for Thought' – You'll see.

HEALING DEVELOPMENT

One night in bed my hands were hot,
Why? I did not know.
A different kind of heat it was
From that which made me glow
And feel warm all over.
This was centred in my hands,
And then my fingertips tingled too –
Wonderment expands!

A visit to Charles Chapman
Gave me a big surprise.
"The gift of healing you have," he said,
"To develop it would be wise.
To be able to help others
Is a truly wonderful thing.
The pleasure you receive from it
Encompasses everything."

My husband too agreed with this,
And with his full support
The decision to go ahead was made.
Enthusiasm caught!
"Spirit works in wonderful ways," was said,
And so it turned out to be,
For all around I soon found
Were Healers advising me.

I'd joined a group of people
So wonderful to know,
A positive attitude to life
Within them all did glow.
Encouragement they gave me
To develop in every way.
Each pathway led to something new
And I learned more each day.

202

This 'work' is really a pleasure
And Spirit is my Guide,
Knowing exactly what has to be done
And always by my side.
For they are happy to use me
As a channel through which to heal
And we do help each other –
It's a complementary deal.